Dr. Arnold of Rugby

The man who changed the face of Education

by

Eileen Elias

Chapbook series published by:

Pipers' Ash Limited

www.supamasu.com

CHIPPENHAM ◆ WILTSHIRE ◆ ENGLAND
SN15 4BW

'Salisbury Edition'
ISBN 1-902628-57-8

Contents

Dr. Arnold of Rugby - The Man Who Changed the Face of Education

Chapter 1   The Youngest of Seven

IN THE LAST YEARS of the eighteenth century, a small boy named Thomas, not yet out of the nursery, was looking forward to his next birthday. What would Papa, a Collector of Customs for the Isle of Wight, give him as a birthday present? A hobby-horse? A hoop to bowl? Or something nearer to his heart - a book? A book would be much more to this small boy's taste, for he was already something of an infant prodigy.

When it came, Papa's birthday present was - not one book, but the whole twenty-four volumes of Smollett's "History of England". And Tom was delighted!

William Arnold and his wife Martha had, from the start, high hopes of their seven children, of whom Thomas was the youngest. There were already two boys in the family: the first-born, called William after his father, and christened, so it was said, twice over in the young parents' excitement; and, later, Matthew. In between came a string of pretty little girls: Martha, known as Patty, Lydia, Susanna and Frances. And now at last came Thomas, whom they all adored: though neighbours sometimes thought this shy little boy, a book-lover from the age of three whose favourite reading was the Bible, rather too much of an oddity.

William and Martha, however, had no fears. They enjoyed their growing family, their "sweet prattlers" as Martha fondly called them. The problem was - where to put them. Now that the seventh had been born, however welcome, their little rented house in Cowes, on the Island, was bursting at the seams. There were the parents, and Martha's younger sister Susan who had come to live with them, and all the children, as well as the two maidservants. By the time Thomas was a year old, his father, by now a Collector of Dues for Trinity House and responsible for the Island's services, had found a more convenient place on which to build a house: a derelict farm site at the other end of the harbour, nearer to his work and with wonderful views of the sea, and twenty-five acres of grass and trees where the children could play.

"One of the sweetest spots in the whole island," wrote Martha, a devoted diarist and letter-writer to friends and family. And since her father and his family, the Delafields, had emigrated to America, William, a keen gardener, took the opportunity of asking for some

American shrubs and seeds for the new garden they were planning together, with individual plots for the children: "any pretty flowers that you think would flourish in this climate without much aid from a hot house". He was determined to make the family home, which he called Slatswood, the best possible place in which to bring up his brood. He little knew how much influence it would have on the youngest child, Thomas, the future Headmaster of Rugby.

Such were the scenes against which young Tom would pass his childhood, in the fine new house with its acres of land, overlooking the sea and all that went with it: the busy life of the harbour, the vessels sailing along the Channel, the cargoes from foreign lands, the troop ships and convoys -for this was the time of the Napoleonic Wars, when all England was expecting invasion at any moment. Indeed, there was a period when Martha considered following the example of some of her neighbours and evacuating her young family to the mainland, for rumours of the war were rife, and the little Island was highly vulnerable. Had she done so, young Tom would have been deprived of much that was to be useful to him in later years: the chance to study both history and geography and to impart a realism to his teaching that would remain in the thoughts of his pupils long after they themselves had left school.

But Martha preferred to stay with her growing family, and Thomas's interest in the vivid scenes grew year by year. William devoted as much time as he could spare to giving lessons to his young enthusiast, in a form the child could understand and enjoy. Together they filled an exercise book - still extant - with notes and coloured drawings of the ships of the Royal Navy and the various flags carried by the vessels from foreign parts; whilst at home he devoted time to showing Tom portraits of famous men and linking the pictures to events in history. Aunt Susan, too, gave the child lessons in geography by means of geographical cards, first of the counties of England, and later those of the world. Occasional "prizes" for Tom's successes came to him in the form of books, always his favourites, and long before he was six he had collected quite a number of volumes, including the "History of Rome" in two parts, while his brother Matthew wrote to him from boarding school with help with his Latin declensions.

In spite of - or perhaps because of - all these achievements, the little boy was not popular amongst the neighbours around Slatswood. He was a reticent child with little conversation, that is, until people really got to know him. Though he loved the lively garden games he played with his brothers and sisters during their holidays, and was full of ideas for

6

mock battles on the Slatswood estate (after the Classical style of Greece and Rome, as befitted a young Classical scholar), he was by no means popular with the neighbourhood children, and mostly silent when visitors came. Yet this very experience was to enable him, in later years, to deal gently and with sympathy towards many a shy "new boy" of nine or ten, homesick and miserable in his first term, entering the rough and tumble of life at Rugby.

Certainly the young child was well advanced before he was six, and even composed a blank-verse tragedy to read to his parents. But tragedy of a different kind came to the family when his father, who had often disregarded signs of fatigue and ill-health, was suddenly overtaken by illness and died in a few hours, shortly before Tom's sixth birthday, from an attack of angina pectoris.

Martha, his wife, was completely overcome at the sudden end to their family happiness. Left alone with her sister, threatened by the thought of having to sell their beloved Slatswood and move to cheaper lodgings, she sought help from wherever she could, and was about to confide in her family for financial assistance when she was unexpectedly offered the position of Postmistress of the Isle of Wight. Though fairly conversant with these duties through her marriage to William, she would not be awarded the salary of a male Postmaster. But it was just enough to enable her to finish the education of the three children still at boarding school, and to remain in the family home.

Susanna, Frances and Matthew were the ones most in need of help, to continue their education away at boarding school - though poor Susanna was already showing signs of ill-health, and was later to become a complete invalid. There remained the young Thomas, and though he loved his lessons at home, with no father to guide him he would surely need more schooling than Slatswood could give him. He, for his part, was ready and willing to travel to the mainland to continue his studies as soon as a boarding school could take him. He had outgrown the nursery.

Indeed, he had been highly indignant when Matthew, in a letter from school, had inquired whether his young brother still wet his trousers!

And so it was, some two years later, that Martha and Susan accompanied eight-year-old Thomas to Southampton to join the chaise that was to take him to Lord Weymouth's Grammar School at Warminster.

Chapter 2 Thomas At School

YOUNG THOMAS must have been by far the youngest passenger that autumn day on the chaise that carried travellers from Southampton to Warminster. His mother and Aunt Susanna had travelled from the Island to the mainland to see him safely off for his first "Short Half" at school, the traditional school year at that time being divided into two, the "Short" and the "Long" terms; but from now onwards their beloved small boy must travel alone. Eight years old and full of enthusiasm, Tom was quite ready for his first experience of school; nor was it too alarming, for his brother Matthew had been a boarder at Warminster before him, and one or two of the masters there were already on good terms with the Arnold family. But Martha and her sister, as they watched the chaise drive off, had fears for the youngest of their seven. Lord Weymouth's famous Grammar School took boys of all ages, most of them sons of local farmers and minor gentry, and there would be a great difference between an eight-year-old and some of the great husky lads of eighteen with whom he would be sharing daily life, in school and out. Boarding school was then, and had been for many years before, a rough-and-tumble life for younger children used only to the comforts of home.

Thomas, however, was full of joy as the chaise approached the impressive stone buildings of the Grammar School on the Bath Road north of Warminster. He was well ahead in his studies, and anxious to learn more. He would need all his Latin, learnt at home, as soon as the term began, for even the school rules, as he was soon to find, were in Latin - and woe betide the nervous newcomer who found himself unable to quote, still less remember, them one by one. A boy must not talk at meals, must not rip his boots, his cap or other garments - and so on, in bewildering sequence; and the penalties for nervousness or forgetfulness were often extreme.

Boarding schools of this period were notorious for the harshness of regime and the exacting demands of the classroom. Lessons consisted almost entirely of learning by heart and translating the Greek and Roman classics, whilst in the playground and the dormitories for the boarders - for there were day scholars as well - there was no supervision at all.

8

Thomas himself, however, had no such fears. He was looking forward to his first sight of his new school, Lord Weymouth's Grammar School, an impressive stone building on the Bath Road just north of the little town of Warminster.

The headmaster at that time was a kindly man who got on well with his pupils, he even played chess with them and promised a half-crown to any boy who could beat him. Thomas's first letter home is full of happy news. "All the grammer boys are below me," he tells his anxious mother, with little regard to spelling. "I have only got one lesson which I say tomorrow morning." As for the seniors, "I like all the great boys," he tells her, and goes on to relate some exciting playground games of coaches and highwaymen, games which he had often played with his brothers and sisters in the garden at Slatswood.

But things soon changed for the worse. Although the headmaster was gentle and the ushers did their best, the school routine was decidedly harsh. The masters were powerless to enforce order, even in class, while in the playground and dormitories, where the ushers never ventured, chaos could - and often did - reign supreme.

Added to this, young Thomas was finding it difficult to make friends. A studious child, who actually enjoyed his work and was already far ahead of his fellows, he was not at all popular either with the boys or with the ushers, with the exception of the Reverend James Townsend Lawes, who was already well known to the family and proved quite happy to go for long walks with his new pupil and occasionally help him with his spelling lessons.

Thomas's letters home during his second term were not nearly so happy. "This is such a stupid place," he wrote dispiritedly in the April of 1804. Such is the penalty of being a scholarly child, far above the level of his schoolfellows, a boy who loved books more than ragging, and it was not easy for him to make friends.

However, as usual, he knew how to come to terms with such a situation, and did in fact join many of the boys' activities. Being a lover of the outdoors, he found his pleasures in exploring the countryside, taking part in long walks and fishing expeditions, and organising playground "battles" with the other lads, although Thomas, being what he was, usually modelled these on the classical lines of Homer rather that on the current events of the day, like the bitter war with Napoleon which was actually going on at the time.

He was by now gradually making friends amongst others of his age, who in turn were beginning to understand this odd little boy with his unnatural taste for Caesar's Commentaries. "I can almost recite them without recourse to my dictionary," he tells his mother with pride. His playground games - notably his version of the Siege of Troy - were beginning to gain him popularity. "I feel very happy and comfortable," he now writes home, adding with due formality, "a circumstance which I am sure you will be very much delighted to hear."

School work at Warminster, as at most schools of the time, consisted almost entirely of studying the Classics, together with ancient history, which of course came easily to the young scholar, though gruelling enough to the rest. But outside lesson time, Thomas was beginning to enjoy life more freely. Dancing classes, almost a necessity for a well-brought-up young gentleman of the time, interested him greatly, although on one occasion when the headmaster chose to pay a visit to the lesson, he became, as he confessed in a letter home, "very awkward with my steps". Mealtimes were also popular with a small boy always hungry. "I stuffed as full as I could hold," he wrote home cheerfully, "with cake, tea and plumb pudding."

Like all the boys, with expenses at the pastrycook's ever increasing, Thomas's letters home contained pleas for more pocket-money. Such demands often exasperated his generous Aunt Susanna, to whom he was constantly in debt. At one time the poor lady was provoked to speak her mind, demanding a detailed explanation as to where and when her money had gone. What resulted was Thomas's indignant reply in carefully considered phrases just this side of rudeness: "You desired me to inform you how I came to spend so much money. In the first place," he wrote - and the epistle goes on to cite in detail his weekly expenditure with friends at the tuck shop. "Now consider," he points out, "how this must impair my purse." "In the second place," he continues, and then follows a long list of school expenses at mealtimes, including "eggs every morning, either one or two, which cost a penny a piece," and concludes with charming impertinence, "I hope I have now cleared myself to your satisfaction." Young Thomas was getting too big for his boots.

In other ways, too, the young scholar was fast maturing. He enjoyed the Classics, but was already becoming critical of their legacy. "I am quite tired," he wrote home like any bored professor, "of the pompous boasts which are everywhere to be met with in Classical writers," adding "especially Cicero." He was beginning to criticise even his teachers. Of Gabell, under whom he studied, he reported: "I think that Mr Gabell hardly makes sufficient allowance for boys defective in capacity," adding "I verily believe that half at least of the Roman history is, if not totally false, at least scandalously exaggerated." In addition he had already begun to look outwards at the state of affairs on the political scene and to question issues of the Napoleonic Wars and the subject of pacifism - resulting in a worthy twenty-two line poem of his own on the subject of the Quakers, beginning;

"How bless'd is he who leads a Quaker's life,
Secure from anxious care and void of strife....."

although he was never to adopt pacifist principles himself.

In fact the Battle of Trafalgar and the death of Admiral Nelson deeply affected the growing boy. He was also beginning to think seriously about his future. The Bible was still his favourite reading, and already at the age of eleven he was contemplating entering the priesthood. "I am so attached to that life, "he wrote in serious mood to his family at Slatswood, "that I could not endure any other."

The sole objection he had to the priesthood involved a difficulty he retained all his life - that of getting up in the morning. Early rising, so necessary for any church service, filled him with fear, and indeed could have seriously impeded his promotion to the priesthood. Even at school he had difficulty in getting up at the sound of the rising bell, - not surprisingly, since the boys were expected to be up at 5.30 and ready for two hours or so of lessons before breakfast, a common custom at the time.

Thomas had clearly outgrown his little school at Warminster, and at home at Slatswood his mother and aunt were making plans for his future education. A public school was clearly advisable, as his father had always hoped; but how were two ladies with little money between them to pay the much heavier expense of five or six years of boarding education at one of the traditional schools?

In the event, Martha and Susanna between them were able to raise just enough money to pay for Thomas's fees as a Commoner at Winchester, since it was obvious that the boy could in due course obtain a scholarship there. In addition, as Mr Lawes and Mr Griffith, both Wykehamists, informed his mother, there was already a traditional link between Lord Weymouth's Grammar School and Winchester.

The school did not demand an entrance examination. Pupils were admitted by election, provided a vacancy occurred. From this they could proceed to the position of Scholar, the fees then being not so far removed from those at Warminster. Nevertheless Martha and her sister had serious doubts about the boy's future at such a school. Everyone knew that life for a new boy there would include plenty of bullying: the young victims had to be prepared for a tough existence without any hope of supervision from the ushers, who took no notice of what was going on in the playground or in the crowded dormitories. Most public schools of the time were the same: nor was the fault with the boys alone. At Eton, the famous "Flogger Keate", who ruled with the birch and was feared by all his pupils, was still the headmaster.

But since Thomas was already set on entering the Church, it was evident that an education at Winchester, William of Wykeham's foundation, which would lead on to New College, Oxford under the same endowment, could be to young Thomas's advantage. And so in due course it was with hopeful hearts that the two ladies from Slatswood saw their young charge off, curly-headed as ever and still looking extremely young, for his first half at Winchester, just after his twelfth birthday.

Thomas at twelve was apparently an easy victim for bullying at his chosen school, and on his very first night, as he knelt to say his prayers in the crowded dormitory, suffered the usual volley of boots flung at him from every quarter. Indeed, his sufferings there were still not forgotten when it came to his headship at Rugby, where such atrocities were still in vogue on his accession. One of his first acts was to make himself accessible as headmaster and comforter to any boy, newcomer or not, who wanted a word of encouragement.

At Winchester Thomas was soon put through the traditional horrors that befell a new pupil of twelve or so. Amongst these was the cruel ceremony of the Tin Gloves. A terrified child was questioned: had he brought with him his Tin Gloves? On receiving a bewildered shake of the head, the boy was made to hold out both hands, on the backs and fronts of which were drawn lines with a red-hot poker fresh from the fire. Thus tortured, he was told by his jeering tormentors that the painful blisters would harden, thus avoiding the need for the "tin gloves".

This was but the beginning of vicious cruelty on the part of the seniors towards their nervous young fags. Every boy in the Lower School was made a fag, at the mercy of the older boys who sent them on numerous errands at any time of the day, mealtimes included, so that their young lives were perpetually interrupted on pain of beatings from the seniors. Tearful new boys were tossed in blankets, roasted before the fire, thrashed with ash canes, locked in cupboards and chests, without mercy; and young Thomas was obliged to suffer with the rest.

Discipline out of school was supposed to be the province of the so-called prefects or praepositors, who were expected to keep order, but this system more often encouraged the older lads to dominate the younger ones, often to the point of cruelty. Indeed the prefects themselves were sometimes paid an annuity, which did nothing to moderate their interference, not only out of school but during long periods of prep - or "Books" as it was known - where they were left completely in charge.

In addition to bullying, the boys at Winchester were subjected to a routine hardly credible to us, though common enough in the public schools of the time. They were expected to be up by 5.30 and in chapel by 6, followed by three hours of lessons on empty stomachs for four days a week. Every pupil - and some were only eight or nine years old - studied a curriculum consisting almost entirely of Latin and Greek, herded together in one enormous schoolroom with the headmaster at one end and the usher at the other. So crowded was this schoolroom that a number of pupils could not even find a seat, as is shown in engravings of the time, and had to study as best they could by leaning against walls and desks.

Lesson time over, they would break off for half an hour for breakfast consisting, according to one pupil, of "bread, stinking butter and beer or milk". That finished - interrupted by the forays of seniors after the fags -the school reassembled to compose their Latin verses until twelve o'clock break-time. On free days the whole school escaped to a grassy area a mile away known as the Hills, where for half an hour or so they could engage in mimic battles or ball games. Then it was back for a small lunch consisting, we are told, of "bread and cheese with plumb pudding on Fridays and Saturdays, and beef on Sundays", that is, if they were lucky enough to escape the demands of the fifth and sixth form prefects, who seldom left their fags enough time to enjoy their meal.

After lunch, unless a holiday, the boys settled down to another four hours of strenuous preparation, with a quarter of an hour's break for "beevers" - bread and beer. At six o'clock they were free at last for the main meal of the day: dinner, consisting of a joint, "mouldy bread" and beer, the beer being necessary to avoid the frequently contaminated water of the times.

In spite of this rigorous regime and the horrors of fagging, young Thomas managed to settle down and even make friends - in particular one who later was to marry his sister. He flung himself enthusiastically into the outdoor life of the school, going on long walks, swimming, fishing and generally enjoying himself as he had as a child at Slatswood. His fellow scholars managed to come to terms with this scholarly new boy who actually liked the Classics, and so no doubt could offer a helping hand to others at preparation time, for Thomas was no swot. Indeed he found work so easy that he had plenty of time for other activities, and was even found breaking the rules by playing a forbidden game of cards, though he escaped punishment by immediate confession of his crime. Perhaps his curly hair and boyish complexion played their part, for his position in class was far ahead of his years.

Thomas was already finding his feet, though he did not escape the usual bullying in the dormitory where he slept with nine others. However he was reasonably content, and was soon able to write home: "I am as happy as I could be at any school, and would certainly be unwilling to make a change with any." Which must have been good news for his worrying mother and aunt at Slatswood.

In his first year Thomas was actually chosen to take part in Winchester's traditional "Commoners Speaking", due to his incipient powers of oratory. He seems to have thoroughly enjoyed the occasion once he had got the better of his initial nervousness. He described it in detail to his family at home: "It is natural to suppose that all the school were in their best array. I was drest as follows: breeches (cords) with their strings tied in my very best manner (bad, I am sure is the best you will say), white cotton stockings, clean shoes (rather a rarity), my best blue waistcoat and best gown, a clean neckcloth and band, and hands washed as white as ever Lydia's (his sister's) are! Well, in this dress I had to speak before Officers, Prebends, the Warden, Fellows, Masters, Tutors and I don't know who besides. I was never so frightened in all my life.... but rewarded by an excellent dinner: mock-turtle soup, veal cutlets, asparagus and marrow puddings. I suppose you will say that I "am always caring about my inside" - here he describes the food again - "and am growing so bulky that I crack my breeches very frequently."

All this was followed, as usual in Tom's letters home, by a polite request for more pocket-money (seven guineas a term, he suggests) from his long-suffering Aunt Susanna.

Out of doors the scholars enjoyed a considerable amount of freedom. Thomas joined enthusiastically in whatever was the sport of the moment, and occasionally in the usual boyish pranks - such as throwing their straw hats into the river and watching to see which one would be the first to sink. Indoors, too, Thomas was becoming quite popular, re-enacting the many amateur theatricals enjoyed by the Arnold family at home. Saturday evening performances in College "chambers" were always popular. Thomas would help to improvise curtains and stage, making use of the dormitory furniture and providing seating, the prefects on forms, the rest of the audience on chairs, beds or the tops of cupboards.

He even became accustomed to the ragging which frequently took place in the dormitories with so many boys penned together without supervision. Though he hated the bullying, he nevertheless managed to survive the complete disorder of those nights when the boarders apparently went mad, breaking windows, throwing dirty slops in the faces of their assailants, and hurling missiles, wherever they could find them, at anybody in their way. In one instance Thomas himself was hit by a stone washing-box, so severely that his head received considerable injury, but he was able to send a wry message home: "My pericranium being far harder than any stone, the washing-box rebounded"- and he was left with only a cut.

Indeed Thomas was finding life, even under Spartan conditions, at least tolerable and at most quite enjoyable. As he wrote to his old teacher Mr Lawes at Warminster, "Everything is now easy to me, though I confess I found some difficulty at first."

Thomas was doing well in his studies, as befitted a young man preparing to go on to university, although the conditions for work were often harsh. After hours of evening "Books"the boys were expected to attend chapel at eight, after which it was frequently necessary for them to finish the next day's preparation in bed at night. Each bed had a shelf above it, to accommodate books for nightly study: many boys, simply in order to keep their place in form, were obliged to work well into the night, or else - as Thomas often did - wake early to prepare the lesson for the next day. The penalty for bad work was often extreme: anything from six to sixty strokes with the so-called "Bibling Rod" applied by the headmaster each morning, arrayed in ceremonial robes and cocked hat, on the bare backs of any unlucky scholar who could not repeat his lesson. This was not often Thomas's fate, for he was already finishing his studies and beginning to think seriously about the future.

Thomas, though not yet sixteen, was certain that he wanted to enter the ministry. He was already critical of the clergy, denouncing the "nefarious forgeries and worldly conduct of the Christian bishops" (harsh words from a schoolboy!) and felt he could improve matters. "Hereafter," he wrote solemnly," in mature age (and God grant I may), I will perhaps more warmly undertake the cause."

And so at last, barely sixteen, Thomas fulfilled his ambition and, following the custom of a Wykehamist, went up to Corpus Christi, Oxford, where his brother Matthew had studied before him.

Chapter 3 Oxford and Beyond

A WONDERFUL NEW WORLD opened for young Thomas Arnold when he went up to Corpus Christi and found - freedom at last! The very air of Oxford breathed freedom: his own rooms, his own belongings around him; lectures to attend, walking through the cobbled streets of Oxford, passing the great dome of the Radcliffe Library, glancing up at the steeple of the University Church of St Mary's, gazing down the gentle curve of the "High", lined with dignified college buildings, passing under the gate of Corpus into the quadrangle where the mythical pelican, carved in stone, perpetually feeds her young.

Like any young freshman, Thomas went shopping in the town, buying china and glasses and candlesticks - "a very neat set of things" as he wrote home to the family, generous Aunt Susanna having, one may be sure, proffered the money. His precious books he set on the table - "in battle array", conscious that they gave his college room "a very literary appearance".

From the first Thomas felt at home in this new life, sampling it to the full. A number of his friends were also up at Oxford, and breakfasts at their colleges, or "drinking tea" at his own, made a pleasant break from the necessary studies. Thomas was determined to work as hard as he could with his goal before him: a first class degree, leading to the ministry - although he was not quite so sure now of certain beliefs which troubled him from time to time. But for the moment, all he wanted in life was here in this enchanting city.

Thomas enjoyed making new friends and taking great walks into the pleasant Oxfordshire countryside, so different from his own. The river, as always, was one of his greatest joys. He found it "most pleasurable" to row a light skiff on voyages of discovery up the Cherwell, often with friends, amongst whom was one John Buckland, who, though he never guessed it, would one day marry his sister. "My way of life," he wrote home, "suits me exactly. I have every convenience and comfort and can be either alone or in society, just as I please."

Work, however, was exacting. Corpus was a small, intimate college, but it set high standards. Thomas was used to working hard: his world was the world of books, and he had an aim in view - the coveted "First". Long hours were spent at his desk or in the lecture rooms, and as the years went on there were moments when he complained that he had no free time: "I am obliged literally to read Aristotle with my breakfast", and again, "No time to myself. I am indeed become a hermit and never show my nose in Oxford till it gets dark."

Great discussions, however, took place within the College throughout his days there, and though he was so young and innocent-looking - an undergraduate at sixteen - his contributions were well received. He did not mind being dubbed a Jacobin for his views, and his forthright manner of speech soon came to be accepted. His range of interests embraced almost everything, from the Napoleonic Wars to literature and classical history, and he soon found himself in the company of John Taylor Coleridge, nephew of the poet John Keble, who would later play an important part in his life, and another friend by the name of Penrose.

On his long walks Thomas was frequently accompanied by John Buckland, and together they explored the local countryside, with its fine mansions at Blenheim and Nuneham Courtenay. Strangely enough, the romantic venue of Godstow, the ruined nunnery beside the Trout Inn, itself a favourite haunt of young men, failed to impress him. Built by "Edith ye Prioress" in the year 1138, it still stands in a field by the waterside, but to Thomas the scenery seemed dull and uninteresting - "not a tree to be seen except for a few stunted ugly elms". But the long walks with Buckland relieved the strain of his studies, and in the May of 1840, three weeks before his 19th birthday, he found himself with his coveted "First" in Literae Humaniores, the classical degree.

"Eight o'clock in the evening," he wrote home on the 24th of May. "The Class paper is just published, and Penrose and myself are in the lst Class," adding a heartfelt sentiment: "All is as I could wish."

Free at last to enjoy himself, Thomas set out for a well-deserved holiday break, accompanied by his friend Penrose. As usual, it was a walking tour, along the valley of the Wye, which was, to romantically-minded young people of the time, a miniature "Grand Tour". The two walked and walked, from village inn to village inn, down the beautiful River Wye with its high cliffs and tree-lined valleys, no doubt earnestly discussing their future. But for Thomas the immediate future was already ensured: he had done so well in his Finals that, scarcely nineteen, he had been offered a coveted Fellowship at Oriel College, which would take care of his future until the day came when he could, as he had planned from boyhood, enter the Church as an ordained priest.

It was still only summer, and time for Thomas to return home to his family before taking up his prestigious Fellowship, with quarters of his own in the heart of his beloved Oxford. He returned, however, not to the Isle of Wight but to a very different scene. His poor sister Susanna, already showing signs of serious illness, had been taken by her mother to London to consult the doctors there, during which time the young girl was submitted to various painful processes in the hope of restoring her to health. To be nearer to London, Martha and her sister had moved to the village of Kensington, renting a small house within what was known as Pitt's Buildings.

Pitt's Buildings, however, and indeed the village of Kensington itself, did not appeal at all to the young Oxford graduate. True, he was deeply involved with this, his favourite sister, who by now was suffering from paralysis, having lost all power in her right side and in both legs. Only twenty-five, she had become a permanent cripple, and was to remain so for the next twenty years.

Ever affectionate to her brother, Susanna had just managed to compose a letter of congratulation to him on his success, and wrote with difficulty, using her left hand: "That your career through life may be fortunate and honourable, happy and peaceful, and crowned with the first of all blessings, health, is the fervent wish and prayer of my dearest Tom's most affectionate, attached sister and friend, Susanna Arnold." A touching letter, still preserved, which Thomas treasured to the end of his life.

From the first Thomas disliked Kensington, "quite a mongrel," as he dubbed it, "half town, half country", though acknowledging that for his sister's sake it was the only possibility. "There is nothing in the world for me to do, nothing to induce me to stir out by myself" - a common enough experience for a young man just down from Oxford and plunged into family life against his will. However, he had to accept that here he would spend his vacations for the next two years or so, far removed as it was from the hallowed ground of Oriel. To him it appeared "a vile hole", and he tried his best to enliven the days with some of his Oxford friends, exploring London with his sisters Frances and Lydia, and his young cousin Joe Delafield.

Already the young man from Oxford was popular with the ladies. He writes of brief encounters with attractive young women like one Miss Burley -"very pretty and not very reserved, neither is she over much troubled with sense" - and a certain Miss Ormerod, "who is, I think, sensible and of most excellent principles, but rather reserved in company." But it was too early yet to think of engagement or marriage:

18

there was the whole of London to visit with his various friends, the Victory parade to witness in the spring of 1814, when the town went wild over the Duke of Wellington's recent victory over the French, and sister Lydia's unexpected marriage to the Earl of Cavan in the August of 1814 - quite an occasion.

Then there were the increasingly frequent visits by Thomas's Oxford friend John Buckland, who apparently did not share Thomas's dislike of the village of Kensington. Indeed, his visits became so frequent that it was no surprise when sister Frances shyly announced their engagement. John had good prospects: he had already opened a little private school at Hampton on the Thames, and it was he who arranged that Martha and her sister, who could hardly be left alone to care for the invalid daughter, should come and live nearby. Soon, much to Thomas's relief, ugly Kensington was exchanged for the more pleasant riverside, where his mother, aunt and sister had found a house for themselves near to their daughter, known as Hampton Cottage.

Little did Thomas know that this change of scene would affect the whole of his future life, and not only of that, but of generations yet to come.

For the moment, though, he was concerned with his fellowship, which left him comparatively free to pursue studies of his own. There had been only two vacancies at Oriel, and Thomas had scarcely expected an award: many of the other candidates had been better qualified than himself, but Whately of Oriel, on whose opinion the decision rested, felt that though others appeared more "polished", this young scholar from Corpus Christi, young as he looked, had more promise about him: he would soon learn to express himself better.

Whately's opinion was soon shown to be a wise one, when Thomas, the same year, easily won the Chancellor's Latin essay prize, and followed up this success in due course by winning the prize for the best English essay. The labours of his parents and Aunt Susanna in their Slatswood home, the training received at Warminster and later at Winchester, were bearing fruit at last.

Thomas was now expected to reside in College for at least his first year, paying no fees; yet somehow he had to support himself on a comparatively small income. Just on twenty, he found himself enjoying the life of a Fellow, especially since his friend John Keble was there as well, and together they enjoyed the familiar pleasures of Oxford life, bathing in the river, rowing and taking long walks into the countryside - "skirmishing," as Thomas quaintly put it. Theology and the Classics were still the subject of his studies, essential if he were to enter the priesthood, but there was still the question of money. He looked round for something that would bring him in a small income, and decided to take up private tutoring. There were always a good many youths hoping to enter the university who needed coaching - or so he told himself.

In the event, however, the pupils were to prove somewhat elusive. He could not ask for more money from home - "for this I owe to you," he had already told his mother on graduating - and was obliged to borrow from his cousin Joe Delafield, who was working in his father's brewery, in order to make ends meet. Soon, however, he could report that he was "driving four coaches" and the fees were mounting, or rather the bills were mounting as his pupils failed to pay their way. By the winter of 1817 Thomas found himself with five pupils, and was able to allow himself a little latitude. Always an enthusiastic traveller - in his early teens he had visited eight of our most famous cathedrals - Thomas, now that the wars with France were over, took a tour of the battlefields, Brussels, Belgium and the Rhine, and the following two years saw him sailing down the Meuse and the Moselle. Later, he began to explore for the first time the beauties of his own country, the Lakes, and it was here that he first met the poet Wordsworth and began the close friendship with the Lakeland poets which lasted all his life.

By 1818, however, Thomas was beginning to wonder whether he was really fitted for the life of a priest. He had had doubts before, chiefly about the nature of the Trinity; but his reforming zeal had put these out of his mind. There was so many aspects of the priesthood which he felt obliged to challenge, but was he the right man to do it? He consulted the Bishop of Oxford, who advised him to stay the course: every young man had doubts, and his faith would overcome them. However, Thomas was still troubled in mind. There were the Thirty-Nine Articles to be sworn to, and he doubted whether he could manage that.

In the December of 1818 Thomas found himself ordained as a deacon in Oxford's beautiful old Cathedral, the first step towards the ministry. Now he could rightly describe himself as the Reverend Thomas Arnold and add to this the title of Master of Arts. For a young man he had already come a long way. Yet six months later, he found himself still at Oxford, having finally decided that the priesthood was not for him. A childhood fear of getting up in the morning still haunted him: how could he ever manage those dreaded early services? It seemed a trivial matter enough, but he knew now that his doubts were deeper. There must be some other path for him to follow. What else was there to show for all those past years of earnest study? "I feel I should never be a barrister," he told his friends and family. Teaching would bring him in some steady money: he was already somewhat experienced. His friends urged hm on. They knew his reforming spirit: could he not reform, if not the Church, at least the current system of education?

It was here that his brother-in-law and old friend John Buckland was to come upon the scene. He had already built up his little school at Hampton, a modest enough establishment, held in one room of the old vicarage in the village, mainly for the sons of local clergy. Buckland had views of his own: he saw the need for a decent education for younger boys from good families, to be prepared for public school and university, and probably for the priesthood. Children at the time had to choose between home tutoring, not always easy to arrange, and the local grammar school, which catered largely for the sons of local gentry or the farming community. Here at Hampton, Buckland had already begun to bridge the gap. What he envisaged was a new type of "preparatory" school where pupils could board, for a fee, and be taught with the public schools in view.

His views now were taking him further. Could he not expand his little school to include a larger establishment, where his pupils could continue the classical education needed for university? Here was his friend, coming to the end of his Fellowship, returning to this new family home at Hampton and wondering what to do. He put the idea to Thomas, and Thomas agreed. They could work together, find a better venue than the one room in the vicarage, set up a school together, in one big house or perhaps two adjoining ones, and advertise it to parents. Thomas could teach the older pupils, aged from eleven or twelve: John could teach the younger ones. Expenses and profits could be worked out and shared. Fees would be seventy guineas a year for the younger boarders, eighty for the older; there could be an entrance fee of ten guineas, and they might also offer the "extras" deemed necessary for a young gentleman - French, perhaps dancing. Pupils could bring their own towels, a knife, and a silver fork and spoon. By the summer of 1819 all was arranged: the only thing left to do was to find suitable accommodation.

The two set out with high hopes. Surely there must be some large house - a vicarage, perhaps, or a small manor house - roomy enough to accommodate two adjoining schools? Their first efforts came to nothing. The two began to seek further afield, in Kent and Surrey. John had his newly married wife to consider: Thomas had his mother, aunt and invalid sister. They were growing dispirited. "I begin to think," wrote Thomas to his friends, "that our school is hopeless."

At long last the two discovered the village of Laleham, on the river, near Staines, where there were two adjoining houses to rent on a long lease. One belonged to an East India captain, the other to a local doctor. The first was ideal, in that it had a large garden which could serve as a playground, whilst the second, though damp and in poor condition, had what could serve as an excellent schoolroom, whilst the outer buildings and coach-house could be repaired and converted into a dining room. The two friends were delighted. They would need to make many repairs, but it would be worth it. Working together, they managed to fit out their new building, and Thomas, in the larger house, made arrangements for his mother, aunt and sister to come and share it, Martha and her sister travelling by chaise, whilst poor invalid Susanna was obliged, in her sad condition, to travel by water - "carried in her crib to and from the boat on men's shoulders". By the summer of 1819 Thomas, now 24, was taking on a new experience, little knowing that it would prove to be his entire life's work.

The house at Laleham, once it had been repaired and re-painted, seemed ideal for a little school. It was a handsome stone building in eighteenth century style, with a portico, tall windows on two floors, and five attic bedrooms for the boarders. Set a little way back from the road, sheltered by tall trees, to the new teacher it must have appeared ideal after the trials of the Kensington village. Next door was the junior school, housed in not quite such dignity but enthusiastically repaired and furnished by John Buckland in his spare time. Thomas, once settled in with his family round him, found his daily routine quite pleasant. No more early rising at five-thirty; he was"down every morning by seven. "I remain by myself in peace," he records, "till eight, then work with them all till nine or half-past. Immediately after breakfast I go down to school and scold and cuff away till about two." (We may take it that the scolding and cuffing was not too severe.) Then, when we have no half-holiday, we work again before dinner for another hour or hour and a half, and then I and my youths go down to Buckland's for dinner, but return for tea, and we always have tea up in the drawing-room with my mother, aunt and Susanna." A comfortable arrangement, which speaks volumes for Thomas's attitude to his young pupils.

"After tea," he continues, "the youths generally write exercises, so that I have a tolerably free evening; and the last thing I do before I go to bed is to take the round of their rooms and see all safe."

Laleham village proved to be a small, scattered one, liable to flooding by the river, and Thomas soon found that most of the inhabitants who could afford it had moved further away. The little church stood forlorn; the services were few and far between, and the Sunday school was pitiful, the teacher there, he was told, being more often drunk than sober. Not surprisingly, the vicar of nearby Staines proved only too pleased to let Thomas and Buckland, as deacons, take the Laleham services in turn, and often the Sunday school as well.

Thomas at first was uncertain about this arrangement. "To say the truth," he admitted, already tired from his labours, "our school is a sufficient dose for anybody; still, I hope bye-and-bye we shall feel our way in the parish a little."

Somewhat later he confessed to a friend that he was coming to feel that Buckland liked the life better than he did: "Not that I dislike being in the school, but quite the contrary; still, however, I have not the experience in that sort of work, nor the perfect familiar with my grammar requisite to make a good master," but added after some thought, "I feel more confidence in myself than I did at first."

As a teacher, he soldiered on, despite initial uncertainty. It was all very different from his quiet Oxford life: he was not coaching scholars on the brink of university, but lads of twelve or so, who needed control as well as teaching. Indeed, in due course he was invited to apply for a teaching post at his old school, Winchester. It was a tempting offer, but he declined it. "The appointment is one which, for the first place, I know myself very ill-qualified to fill, and it would, besides, completely upset my scheme which I have found for my future comfort in life - " and added, significantly, "to enable me to live with economy as a married man."

For by this time Thomas had met and was rapidly falling in love with one Mary Penrose, a young lady who, like himself, came from a big and happy family, and lived in the remote village of Fledborough, a lonely spot near the river Trent in Nottinghamshire.

Mary was the sister of one of Thomas's Oxford friends, young Trevenen Penrose, four years older than Thomas. They had first met when he was on a visit with Trevenen to the family home at Fledborough. Mary was the youngest of five sisters, older than her brother by some two years; she had been brought up in Cornwall, but her father, the Reverend John Penrose, though offered the living in Nottinghamshire, could not bring himself to leave his beloved rocky, sea-girt home in Cornwall till some eighteen years later. In the February of 1801, however, the Reverend Penrose made the final decision to move, and the family, the little girls in tears, packed up and said a sad goodbye to their old home, and were bundled off with all their belongings to their new home, the Rectory at Fledborough.

At first it had not been a happy time for ten-year-old Mary. The village was small and lonely; the February floods were out, and the adjoining flat fields were unimpressive. However, they were a cheerful family, and in time settled down. Some years later, dark-haired Mary, now twenty-seven, first met Thomas when her brother brought him home on a visit at New Year, 1817. She had had her share of sadness, for her mother had only recently died, but Mary had a resilient nature, and it had been a happy time with the young schoolmaster who had joined so gladly in their New Year celebrations.

The two found they had much in common. Both came from large families, both enjoyed simple pleasures, games and singing and amateur theatricals. Thomas told her about his plans for the new school at Laleham and Mary listened with interest; but when it came to serious thought, Thomas had to face up to facts. He had but a small income, and many debts, having been forced to take out a huge loan of some thousand pounds, at five per cent interest, to underwrite his new venture at Laleham. But the next time he came to Fledborough, in the August of 1819, he was ready to ask for Mary's hand in marriage; not without misgivings, as he wrote to a friend: "All is very uncertain."

However, all turned out for the best. The Reverend Penrose received him politely enough, and Mary already knew her own mind. "Nothing could exceed the kindness of the whole family," Thomas was to write a month later from Laleham, "from Mr Penrose downwards - and after, a week of such happiness as I never experienced. All was decided so speedily and so fully that it rushed by me in the acting like a dream, and ever since my life has been something so new to me that I almost seem bewitched altogether, and half expect to wake some morning and find myself at Hampton with no house, nor school, nor prospect of a wife."

Truly, a young man in love.

The next time they met, in mid-winter, Fledborough was snowbound. The Penroses themselves were cut off by floods, which did not recede until February; and Mary had as yet to meet her future husband's family. At the end of February 1820 it was arranged for the Reverend Penrose, Mary and her elder sister Lydia to travel down to Laleham, her brother, now a curate, joining them for a few nights from Eton. Mary, new to the family and to the district, was distinctly nervous, and, tired out with travelling, on meeting Martha and Aunt Susanna, was so overcome that she burst into tears. But it did not take long before she felt quite at home. Thomas, proud of his wife-to-be and of his new school, took her around to meet his friends and colleagues.

"You may imagine my delight on the Sunday," he wrote later to a friend, "in taking Mary about with me, first to the school, where I made her hear how the children were getting on, then up and down my garden, and then to one of my favourite walks by the river." And "I think," he added at the end, "that there could not have been a happier party... It was quite delightful to have them all around me at my own home, and to see them so comfortably associating with my own relations. The Trade (as he called his new profession) "is now flourishing; we have 19 boys and 7 pupils." He had forgotten already that he was still deeply in debt!

Not long after this happy reunion, Matthew, Thomas's elder brother, died. He had been chaplain to the Army of Occupation after the victory of Waterloo, and on his return to England was drowned at sea when his boat capsized. Nor was that the only loss. Martha's uncle, Joseph Delafield, who had so long advised her on her financial affairs, also died, leaving Thomas, the youngest, in fact head of the family. But talking all this over with Mary, the two decided that come what might, debts and all, they would marry as soon as possible. For his own family, Thomas now rented a house next door to the Bucklands, which conveniently became vacant, and left instructions to Martha and Susanna to move in. As for himself, he could wait no longer. Already the summer holidays were upon them. Thomas made their wedding arrangements and then left his mother and aunt to move in, while he and his bride-to-be went back to Fledborough for the rest of the holidays. Thomas, romantically absorbed for the first time in his life, devoted himself entirely to his new love, roaming the countryside, watching the harvesters at work and accompanying Mary about the village. The re-decoration of Martha's house, the arrival of the furniture, even the engaging of a cook, he left to his mother. There was one Phoebe, he wrote, who, he had ascertained, would ask twelve guineas a year plus tea and sugar: would she do? Life was too happy to be bothered about cooks! "I hope some cook will be got before we return, or else our dinner will be in jeopardy!" he added, with the supreme egotism of new love. Yet he could be forgiven.

The pair were finally married in the mid-August of 1820, by Mary's father, at Fledborough's ancient church, set amid trees in the quiet Nottinghamshire countryside. And so Thomas Arnold and his new wife settled down in their home, to a marriage which would be one of the happiest possible. Thomas had settled down to teaching. If he could not accept a clergyman's life, at least he could, as he put it, "use his brains". Teaching the young seemed the best way of doing it, as he was soon to find out.

And so it was that the newly married couple, both looking forward to the future, settled down in their first home together. They seemed an ideally matched pair. Young Thomas was in his prime, full of energy, happy in his unexpected choice of profession; but he knew he needed a partner. He was not one to travel through life alone. Mary, for her part, was a lover of children, brought up in a large and contented family, and looking forward to children of her own. Together they were prepared to work alongside their colleagues, their servants and their pupils. All seemed set for the future, and though they both well knew that they had debts still to be paid, they were quietly determined to get rid of these as soon as possible. In short, the future looked bright.

Above all they shared a profound Christian outlook. In dealing with the boys in their charge, Thomas knew what he wanted: to bring up the young to be God-fearing, above all. Knowledge was one thing, but was worth nothing unless accompanied by a true religious faith, and it was his task to instill it. Together he and Mary studied each child's character, and, as Thomas often said, no pupil could be written off. Finding just one "noble trait" on which to build, all necessary education could stem from that. There was no need to keep talking about religion: any boy who wished was welcome to come and discuss it. Later, as a child matured, his religious education could begin. But as the years were to show, the way to get across to the older pupils was not to badger them with Bible study, but to preach such sermons as they could understand. The personal touch was essential. And, as future events would show, it was to be their headmaster's sermons that would be remembered when lessons were long forgotten. Here in Laleham church, where Thomas was frequently asked to preach, and later at Rugby in the school chapel, his sermons would often prove the turning-point in their young lives.

It was important, then, to establish the right atmosphere in the little school at Laleham of which Thomas now found himself the head. He was largely modelling his views, not on the disciplinarians of Winchester, but rather on memories of that first headmaster at Warminster, who was a friend to the boys, and kindly in disposition - did he not enjoy those games of chess in which he would forfeit half a crown to anyone who could beat him? And with Mary at his side, soon to become the mother of his own children, Thomas could now look forward confidently to the future.

Thomas soon established his own way of running the Laleham school. Apart from breakfast, lessons went on from 7 till 3 p.m. with only a half hour for breakfast. To the traditional subjects of Classics and Divinity, he added some geography and history, which he had learnt as a boy at Slatswood, teaching largely by illustrations and diagrams, as his father had loved to teach him. His lessons were lively, as one pupil attested: "highly praised for their depth and originality". He did not urge on the cleverer boys, but was just as much interested in the slower learners, giving them plenty of time to take in what he taught. The one thing he would never accept was idleness.

Nine hours in the classroom was the usual thing in those days, but out of class Thomas gave himself over to walks with the boys, birds-nesting, catching butterflies, cutting "arrows" from the hedgerows for playground "battles", of which he had always been fond. For dinner he brought his pupils over to Buckland's, where there was a proper dining-hall, joining them at table until it was time to lead them back to his own and Mary's drawing-room to spend the evening. "My pupils all come up to the drawing-room," he told a fellow clergyman, "before tea (which at that time followed the evening meal) "and stay for some time, some talking, some reading, some playing chess or backgammon, looking at pictures etc. - a great improvement if it lasts. If this fair beginning continues, I care not a straw for the labour of the half year, for it is not labour but vexation which hurts a man, and I find my comfort depends more and more on their good and bad conduct. They are my awful charge, but still to me a very interesting one, and one which I could cheerfully pursue till my health or faculties fail me."

In short, Thomas had now found the road along which he would travel, though little did he know to what heights it would lead him.

Chapter 4　Arnold the Teacher

AS IT TURNED OUT, Thomas's marriage to Mary was the beginning of the happiest period in his life. The two were well suited: Thomas ardent and kindly, Mary, gentle and a lover of children. Thomas needed a wife to share his problems, and Mary was always there to do so. Each respected the other, as they did the servants and pupils - a sound foundation for the future.

Thomas now had the incentive he needed for his teaching. For its basis he took Christianity in its widest form. He wanted each pupil to take a pride in himself, each, from the youngest up, to make a contribution. He studied each pupil's character, to find its "noblest trait", something on which he could build: to grow up "God-fearing" was of prime importance. Second only to this was a wish to see every boy healthy, for this was needed to establish a will to learn. Remembering his own youth on the coast at Cowes, he recognised how important it was to acquire a free and healthy approach to life, on which any future education could be based.

Religion, however, could not be taught as a subject. It had to be conveyed in other ways: by an attitude to life, not by lessons or prayers. To the youngest he never preached; but if a boy wished to talk to him on such matters, he would always be welcome. Every Sunday, however, the boys were expected to attend the village church and listen to the sermon (often his own). Given this basis, the rest would naturally follow.

One of his friends at Oxford who knew him in those days summed his teacher up well as a man of maturity: "He was attached to his family as if he had no friends; to his friends as if he had no family; and to his country as if he had no friends or relations." More than once he was called obstinate; but as Trevenen Penrose once put it, "There never was any personal bitterness in his violence... So far as I know, he never entertained an unkind feeling towards any man. All his vehemence was against principles, not against men."

Thomas soon established a routine for the conduct of his little school. The subjects taught were almost entirely the Classics, though

Thomas did include a smattering of geography and history, both of which he had enjoyed under his family's tuition at Slatswood, and in due course added some mathematics. His lessons were lively, as one pupil attested: highly praised for their depth and originality. In short, Thomas Arnold had found his life's work.

To him, there was no such thing as a "worthless" pupil, unless it was a lazy one. To the backward boys he paid special care, giving them all the time they needed. "Lenience," he once said, "is seldom to be regretted -" a sentiment never to be heard of by teachers of the time. On the other hand, on the slacker he had no mercy, and any boy who preferred playing about to working was asked to leave immediately, lest he should corrupt the others, something which indignant parents sometimes found difficult to understand.

The reputation of this new schoolmaster down in Laleham was quietly spreading. It had been a surprise both to Thomas and Mary when an invitation came to him to come and join the staff of his old school, Winchester. "He had reason to think he would be successful," Mary wrote in her diary," as the person who proved successful said he would not stand against him." This offer Thomas had declined, as it would only be that of an usher. He felt he must be in control, not to be met by "tradition and prejudice" - in the event, a wise decision.

The following year it was decided that Buckland's junior school - the forerunner of the modern preparatory school - should be conducted separately from the senior school under Arnold. "It is satisfactory," Mary wrote in the diary she was now keeping, "to think that such a connection began and terminated with friendliness and goodwill on both sides." Thomas now had nine pupils, and charged quite high fees: £200 guineas for board and tuition a year, but despite the fees, he could soon write: "I have overflowed with applications for pupils", even having to refuse the sons of his own personal friends.

One of his pupils, Bonamy Price, has left a record of his days under the headmastership of Arnold, speaking of the "wonderful tone and feeling at the school: a place where a newcomer at once felt that a great and earnest work was going forward. Every pupil was made to feel that there was a work for him to do; that his happiness, as well as his duty, lay in doing that work well". Bonamy went on to describe the "strange joy" that came over a young pupil "on discovering that he had the means of being useful and thus of being happy". He continued: " His hold over his pupils I know perfectly astonished me. It was not as much an enthusiastic admiration for the genius, or learning, or eloquence which stirred within them: it was a sympathetic thrill, caught from a spirit that was earnestly at work in the world" - a handsome tribute from any pupil with an admiration for his past teachers.

One reason for Thomas's fellow-feeling for his pupils, and theirs for him, was that he had his own large and lively young family about him. Both parents earnestly desired children, and their first child, Jane, arrived within the first year of their marriage. Thomas adored her. "I like to have the little one in my arms," he told friends, "very much indeed." The following year Mary, very pregnant, riding out of the garden gate on her pony, slipped on the ice, and the baby, Matthew, was born prematurely on Christmas Eve. The following year Mary was again pregnant with a second little daughter, who died, but the following March found her with another child, called after her mother Mary, whose arrival caused considerable trouble. Mary described the new arrival in her diary: "Nothing could have been more awkward, as the baby was born prematurely, and the nurse who had been engaged for the occasion was having a few days' holiday in London." Thomas's sister Frances was hurriedly sent for from neighbouring Buckland's, and with the help of a maid, Harriet, little Mary was safely delivered. Two more children, Edward Penrose and William, were born in 1826 and 1828, bringing the family to six, all born within eight years. And Mary and Thomas were devoted to them all.

Somewhere within those years Mary began a journal, a monthly record of her children's doings, to be read perhaps by them in later years. "March 1822: Jane "made her exit from her long robes and her entrance into short petticoats. Often she sits on the sofa by my side, hedged in with pillows, and plays contentedly with my keys and her ivory ring." Young Jane, her father recorded later, had a decided will of her own. He described her obstinacy in refusing to curtsey to her mother: Jane was always a determined child. Made to stand in the corner, "her little heart swelled with pride. It made me think how truly is pride our original and besetting sin from the very first."

Matthew, later to become the poet, was the most unfortunate. At a few months old he was considered "backward and rather bad-tempered" and would not lie flat on his back when having his daily rest. Moreover he tried to walk too soon, resulting in a curvature of both legs before the age of two, for which physicians prescribed the wearing of leg irons. This proved a most unhappy decision, and when the child's misery was followed by a fall from his father's sofa, resulting in a "broken head", the physicians were consulted again. They advised another six months in leg irons, but "the confinement was become so irksome," Mary recorded, "and in every way so disadvantageous to our dear boy that from this time we gradually discontinued them and without any bad effect."

A year later the unlucky child developed a strange throat infection, for which he was, in the manner of the day, treated with the conventional "blister", and to add to their worries, Mary became pregnant again. Mary even felt impelled to compose a letter to her children, as a last farewell, and the following year wrote: "Dare I hope to be again so favoured with a safe birth ...let me only try in all events to keep a trusting and thankful heart."

However, the worst did not happen, and a governess was installed for the older children, to follow the syllabus devised by their father, whilst two nursemaids were engaged to care for the younger children. Their parents, however, still took a lively part in their children's lives. Thomas showed them how to bowl a hoop, and made each one a small private garden to tend as he had done himself as a child at Slatswood. Even swimming lessons were introduced, swimming being for their father a lifelong sport. In the classroom Thomas, somewhat prematurely, introduced the learning of Italian, and was a frequent visitor to the schoolroom, hearing their work and rewarding them, as his father had done before him, with a toy as a reward. But he was not always so serious. In fact he so far forgot his hatred of getting up in the morning by rising early and singing as he ran into the children's bedrooms to pull off the bedclothes while they slept!

Thomas enjoyed accompanying Mary on her morning rides, and was also a keen gardener, "There is always something to interest me," he wrote, "even in the very sight of the weeds and litter - for then I think how much improved the place will be when they are removed!"

But his interests did not only apply to his home. Both he and Mary took seriously their duty to the neighbouring poor. "I have now taken care of the Workhouse," he wrote, and in the February of 1824 he and Mary decided to devote their Thursdays to "seeing more of the poor people". He and Mary called regularly on any cottager who was ill, and sat informally on the edge of the bed to talk to the patient, never failing to shake hands individually with the family.

At home in his study Thomas, ever the student, found time to write on subjects of interest to the papers of the time, read while Mary sewed, and even began a work on the subject of Thucydides, which, in three volumes, took him some ten years to finish. He also embarked on a long "History of Rome" which also took some years to finish. But this to him was always a labour of love. "I worked hard and was well rewarded" was a common comment on his days.

But although he had chosen to teach, the state of the Church was continually on his mind, as it had been for him even as a schoolboy of eleven. "I hope to be allowed before I die," he wrote in 1826, "to accomplish something on Education, and also with regard to the Church, which certainly retains the foundation sure as all other Christian societies except the Unitarians, but has overlaid it with a very sufficient quantity of hay and stubble, which I devoutly hope to see burnt one day in the fire." Already his sermons in Laleham church were showing signs of this tendency, different from the old hackneyed efforts of other local preachers. He never tried to be "literary", but instead preferred to be simple and easily understood.

Although his term-time days were busy, Thomas made up his mind to enjoy his holidays like any schoolboy. "I purposely employ myself," he wrote, "in any hard work during the holidays, to give myself a complete recruiting for the ensuing half year; and it is wonderful what great relief to have no regular writing or reading from morning to night, and to be a great deal out in the air."

On one such holiday he stayed awhile with Coleridge, his Oxford friend, in London, and discussed his work as editor of the "Quarterly Review". Here at Coleridge's home he would sing "The Ship a-Sailing" to the young Coleridge children, who once "encored it so many times that I think Papa and Mamma must have been tired of hearing it!"

Occasionally on these holidays he would visit Oxford, and sometimes the West Country, Yorkshire, and the Lake District, where he called on Dorothy Wordsworth and her brother William at Grasmere, drinking tea with them whilst staying at Ambleside. "I was agreeably surprised by Mr Wordsworth," Mary confided to her diary. "I had somehow expected to see rather a trifling sentimental wild-looking person, instead of which I found him mild and gentlemanly."

Later that month they met the other Lakeland poet Southey, drinking tea at the house in Keswick which he shared with the wife and children of Samuel Taylor Coleridge, who had gone off and deserted his family. Southey had been obliged to support them. "I shall always remember," wrote Mary, "the evening with pleasure. There is at once a gentleness and animation and kindness of look and manner about Mr S.(Southey) which is very pleasing."

Back home, Thomas, ever eager to learn something new, engaged an Italian tutor to help him with the language, and went on a visit to Italy for the fourth time. Later, he also spent time in Rome, no doubt working on his "History". A year or so later he spent his holidays exploring France and Germany, keeping a record of his travels

32

throughout. On these travels Mary preferred to move next door into "the other house" and allow her husband to travel alone. This was no hardship to her. "I am not only reconciled to his taking them (the holidays)" she wrote, "but anxious that he should, since he feels that they enable him to bear the weight of his usual occupations without considering them a burthen."

Her husband in his turn treasured her letters. Once, when away in Edinburgh, he wrote: "Thank you for them both, dearest (two letters in one day) over and over again, and you cannot tell what a delight they are to me. Before we were married, darling, we used to think it often enough to write to one another once a week - but now I think we could write every day, and neither be tired of writing nor of reading."

And with each letter the father wrote a note to each of his children. To Jane: "Mamma will find you Colchester on the map where Papa was when he wrote this letter." To Matt: "I mean to see if I can get you a set of bricks when I come home." To Thomas: "My dear Small Tom, I only send you my love and a kiss, and you won't understand as much as this!"

So even when parted, the family felt themselves together, as they would for the rest of their father's life.

Chapter V   The Great Adventure

IT WAS IN THE AUTUMN of 1827 that Arnold's attention was drawn to an advertisement in the "Times" concerning the headship of Rugby School, where the previous headmaster, Dr Wool, was about to retire after 22 years of teaching. This was something that Arnold, absorbed in running his little school at Laleham, would never have noticed. However, friends persuaded him to think about it. After long consideration, in which Mary was deeply involved, for it would affect the whole family, he decided to take things further, and though there seemed little hope, Rugby being a famous school for which there would be many applications, wrote to put himself forward as a candidate.

Thomas and Mary were very comfortably settled at Laleham, and Arnold's modest little boarding school had already attracted a growing number of applicants, far more than the building could accommodate.

But assuming the leadership of a large and well-established school was not to be taken lightly.

For one thing, Arnold had never considered such a step: indeed, teaching had not even been his first choice as a profession. However, the years at Laleham had shown him that his life work was to lie in education rather than the ministry. For another, Rugby school, it was well known, had for some years been running into difficulties: some said, into a decline. Under Dr Wool, numbers had sadly fallen, and lately the Doctor had been losing his grip on discipline. There had been so much disorder that it had been said that the school had come to be run by the pupils rather than their ushers.

True, discipline in schools of the day had long been harsh, administered by the birch rather than the rules. At Eton, the most famous school of all, Dr Keate was still the reigning Head, and had come to be dubbed "Keate the Flogger" for his brutality. The boys learnt little, and that little under perpetual fear. The birch and the dreaded flogging-block were still the order of the day.

Keate himself was liable to be shouted down by the boys even as he preached the Sunday sermon, and it was said that the pupils had let out rats during chapel services, despite knowing they would be victims of the flogging-block the following morning. Keate himself was only five feet tall and the birch was his chief weapon. Indeed he had once flogged a hundred boys in a single day. On another occasion, being handed a long strip of paper bearing the names of boys about to be confirmed, Keate mistook it for a list of miscreants and flogged the lot!

Such, then, was the scene, not only at Eton but at most of the public schools of the time. At Rugby there had not been quite so much brutality, but Dr Wool had let all discipline go. Arnold knew the problems he would meet, and his own manner of teaching was totally different. He would be faced with huge dormitories and a playground, both completely unsupervised by the ushers; and though some sort of prefect system was in force, it was handed over indiscriminately to a few older boys who terrorised the young fags without mercy.

At the time of his application, Arnold was not fully aware that his reputation for good teaching and good relations with his pupils had spread beyond the limits of Laleham. He was sure that in any case the number of applicants better qualified than himself would put him out of the running: all he had was a first class degree and a fellowship, which he had not followed up, so it was with some surprise that he discovered that Whately, his old tutor at Oriel, called upon for a testimonial, had told the staff at Rugby that here was a man who, if elected, would "change the face of education". Never was there a truer prophecy. Whately, as he had on the occasion of the fellowship, judged by promise rather than performance, and to his great astonishment Arnold found himself elected to the headship of one of the oldest and most historic of public schools, to start in the Short Half of the following year.

And so it was that the Arnold family, with their six small children, the youngest scarcely out of babyhood, arrived with their luggage, their nurse and their governess, at the School House at Rugby, ready to embark on Arnold's great adventure.

At first the dull plains of the Midlands appeared uninviting after the pretty riverside village of Laleham, but the School House at Rugby was large and pleasant, and the children soon settled down. For a young man of only 33 the prospect was challenging, but Arnold was ready for it. He had spent the intervening months planning his strategies, for he knew the problems had to be faced immediately or not at all - and he was ready to attack them.

One of his first tasks on arrival was to challenge the old regime of punishment. If rule he must, he would rule with humanity. Although he was not opposed to the birch when really necessary, it was not the right way of initiating a new regime. The regime itself had to be put right first. Under Wool, discipline had been quite separate from teaching. Out of school hours this had been entirely handed over to the so-called prefects or praepostors, who had abused it completely.

The huge dormitories where pupils slept huddled into communal beds, the playgrounds where bullying was rife, and the terrorising of the "fags" and new boys, would have to go. Arnold began with the dormitories. Out went the communal beds, which only encouraged vice. More privacy for study was the next thing to tackle. Senior boys would have their own private studies, where admission would only be by consent, and even the masters, including Arnold himself, would be requested to knock before entering.

The prefect system, he himself recognised, had its points, but it needed careful construction. Properly run, it might revitalise the whole school. Arnold now proceeded to talk to his senior boys, taking them into his confidence and allotting them responsibilities with the right to discipline the younger pupils in an acceptable way. Thus they would be sharing the life of the whole school, and giving the account of it to the headmaster alone, who would be the final arbiter. There would be no possibility of bullying, inside the school or out. The very fact that their headmaster trusted them put them on their honour to do their job well.

But from the beginning their new headmaster accepted the fact that there were already boys in the school who could ruin all these plans. For one reason or another, they were already bullies, or slackers who could no longer profit from their education. This was a fact that Arnold had anticipated from the beginning. He would have to tackle these disruptive elements if this new freedom could succeed.

Though things had never been as bad as they were even then under Keate, Arnold now decided to expel the most troublesome pupils. He would not countenance the experiences he himself had gone through at Winchester - the boot throwing in the dormitories, the midnight fights, the tortures of new boys with the "tin gloves", the roasting and all the rest. This was an unpleasant duty and Arnold set about it forcibly enough. He promptly expelled the bullies and the wasters who set a bad example to the rest. Amongst those who fell foul of him was George Hughes, the brother of the Thomas Hughes would later be the author of "Tom Brown's Schooldays". However in most cases Arnold bore no grudge against the pupils he expelled. His sole intention was to remove the lads who were not benefiting from their education, or were a bad example to the rest.

Furthermore, though he disliked resorting to physical punishment, he made it a rule to use it as a last resort. Indeed, he was able to write to a friend, the new headmaster of Harrow, in April 1829: "I have so far got rid of the birch that I only flogged seven boys last half year, and the same number hitherto in this. I never did, nor do I believe it can be relinquished altogether - only for grave and repeated offences, and then - phew! - in earnest!"

Even so, beating, whether by himself or by his prefects, was subject to strict conditions. Three strokes were usually sufficient, six the maximum: none of the furious flogging of Eton! In addition, every victim had the right to appeal, although if he lied the punishment was doubled.

Wisely, Arnold made all these decisions publicly, before the whole school, sparing nothing. Any offender about to be expelled would be called out before the rest of the pupils and given his decision on the spot, his luggage packed and sent home the following day. For other offences Arnold worked on an ascending scale, mostly by impositions. About these methods he was perfectly clear: "I have never," he stated, "found it necessary to assume anything of a school manner in speaking to the boys. They mind one's usual tone and manner just as much as if they know they cannot presume upon it." Yet again, recalling his own schooldays: "I believe that boys may be governed or guided by gentle methods and kindness and sympathy, to their better feelings, if you show you are not afraid of them." Instead he preferred to shame them into "repentance", as he put it, although as time went on it was not unknown for this most gentle of schoolmasters to lose his temper when provoked. The Headmaster of Rugby was himself only human!

When a pupil was found unsuitable, in one way or another, to continue at school, Arnold had his own way of dealing with the matter. Long ago at Laleham he had pronounced that "the weeds must be removed to allow the good seeds to prosper", and here at Rugby he followed his own rule. He realised that some boys had simply outgrown their time at school, and these were often the lads who, finding themselves bigger and stronger, were tempted into bullying. Others had not the intelligence to profit from their education: they had reached their potential and were better elsewhere. For these he devised a system of superannuation. He would write to the parents, explaining the matter, and then the boy would simply not return for the following half. There was no disgrace and nothing was said.

But neither did he forget them. To some he even offered free coaching in the holidays; to others, the hospitality of his own holiday home in the Lakes. When a boy was going on to university, he would take special pains to explain the previous expulsion to the authorities. Of one such he wrote privately to the Provost of Oriel, his own old college, telling him "not to scruple to receive" the young man he had just expelled. " He was not a bad fellow at all," he explained, "but had overgrown school in his body before he had outgrown it in wit: he was therefore the head of the younger boys for his strength and prowess and this sort of distinction was doing him harm, so that I advised his father to take him away and to get him entered at the university as soon as possible!"

An acute representation that only a headmaster of Arnold's calibre could ever have entertained. Throughout his teaching years, this was his approach to the problems of troubled youth.

Such reforms as these were naturally not immediately popular. Indeed, as regards expulsion, Arnold in those early days had to face the risk of numbers falling. But he stuck to his guns. People have to learn, he believed, "that the first, second and third duties of a schoolmaster are to get rid of unpromising subjects, otherwise a great public school will never be what it might be - " (i.e. a place of education).

But as time went on, Arnold's policies were seen to work, and work well. By 1832 he had largely completed the reforms he thought most necessary. No new boy had, like himself, suffered boot throwing when he knelt to say his prayers. No boy was unduly punished with the birch, whether by teachers or by prefects. No little fag was subjected to cruelty; no private study was invaded against its owner's will. Two years later the youngest of Arnold's first half had grown to seniority, and the school to which Arnold had come had trebled its numbers. The Great Adventure had been seen to work, and in five years Arnold had transformed the face of Rugby.

These reforms completed, Arnold now felt more free to advance his own concept of a "good education". His goal might be expressed in three ways: boys must be encouraged to be, first, God-fearing, second, gentlemanly, and only third, scholarly. That is not to say that he underestimated the usual subjects of a classical education: rather, that a boy who could not profit from it should not be pushed any further. The role of a public school was to prepare a God-fearing young gentleman for, preferably, a University.

With this in mind, he had already got rid of those pupils who might not fit this pattern: but in a sympathetic way. They simply went back home for the holidays and did not re-appear. Likewise he refrained from over-emphasising the subject of religion with the younger pupils: but allowed them time to absorb the ideals he put before them in his Sunday sermons.

With regard to his second objective, the promotion of gentlemanly conduct, his reforms within the prefect system had already provided a suitable background. But apart from the absence of bullying, Arnold still retained, and would do all his life, memories of his first days away from home. No young boy, he decided, would have to suffer the trauma of home-sickness on joining Rugby. With considerable imagination for a headmaster of the times - or perhaps through talks with his gentle wife - he devised means by which a shy young new boy might come to see him without the teasing or even the knowledge of his schoolfellows.

Understanding the reluctance of such a child to be seen approaching the Headmaster's study, Arnold had some steps made by which a boy might come unseen to the School House when he needed to talk. Further, with a touch of inspiration, probably remembering his childhood interest in naval flags off Cowes, he had a flagpole installed upon the School House roof, which, when hoisted with the Union flag, told the boys that their headmaster was now at leisure and able to receive anyone who might wish for a private talk. The result was immediate: good relations were established with any boy who wished to visit him in private; and not only the agony of homesickness, but many of the worries of schooldays, were put at rest.

His objective of installing the gentlemanly arts was already being reached. Bullying, rough manners and speech, were rapidly becoming unknown. The new prefects, conscious of his trust in them, were rapidly establishing good relations with their fags: each respected the other. There remained the question of scholarship. To this point Arnold now turned his attention. There was no question of interfering with the traditional classical education which would see a young man off into the world, if not to university, at least into the professional classes. But to this, Arnold decided, must, in the advancing Victorian age, be added a moderate amount of other studies.

Scripture, of course, was already included in the religious curriculum, but now a foreign language, in this case French, was to be added, as was a certain amount of mathematics. These, so far, had been considered as an "extra" and taught by unqualified teachers, and the boys usually regarded them as a bit of a joke. Now they were to be taken seriously, taught by permanent masters: French in particular was to be allotted to a special classroom. Though he was well aware of the difficulty of speaking a foreign language (English boys, he considered, would never be able to manage that!), he concentrated on reading and grammar.

Some thought, also, was given to the subject of history. Hitherto history had been purely classical, concerned with ancient Greece and Rome. Now it was to be taken seriously, even if only a subservient subject. Geography, too, was to find a place. Remembering his own youth at Cowes, and the way he had picked up his geography by wandering along the harbourside and noting the flags of the different nations, not to mention the geography cards produced by his Aunt Susan, Arnold taught largely by illustration. "I quite marvel," he once said, "to find in what a state of ignorance boys are at 17 and 18, who have lived all their days in inland country parishes or small country towns."

School began at seven, with prayers and lessons before breakfast, followed on three days a week with more lessons till eleven, and again in the afternoon. On the two other days lessons ended at eleven, as they did also on Saturdays. There was a desk for each boy, which was uncommon at that time. Later, German was added to the curriculum - equally uncommon. The Sixth Form was taken by Arnold himself, but he also took pride in knowing every pupil in every form personally - something few headmasters did. Every boy, too, was examined personally by Arnold once a year, orally in the presence of the form master. We have a personal account by one pupil faced with such an examination: "He stepped just in front and began speaking to me. The effect of words falling so close from that tall gaunt form, which was regarded with awe, was strange enough: the blood flew to my face, my head swam, my eyes were dizzy, and my hearing seemed gone. I was hardly conscious of anything till after he ceased to speak." The scared pupil did not realise he was actually being praised!

Arnold's methods were often quite different with the younger pupils. These he would sometimes even take on his knee, talking to them and explaining the lesson with the aid of picture-books, just as he himself had been taught at six years old by his Aunt Susanna. But with the older pupils he did not mind how long he spent in examining them at the end of each half: indeed, Mary once recorded in her journal that "Thomas had often scarcely time to eat his dinner!" Another innovation was the issue of reports to all parents at the end of each half, and eventually reports from the individual masters. The prize system was also improved. Prizes had previously been awarded only to the top pupils, but Arnold took a different view. Prizes were not over-important. "Mere intellectual acuteness," he averred, "divested as it is in too many cases of all that is comprehensive and great and good, is to me more revolting than the most helpless imbecility". He recognised effort rather than success, occasionally, when he saw a pupil taking great pains to improve his work, slipping an extra "prize" from his own pocket into the pocket of the scholar.

Added to which, Arnold delighted, every now and again, to recognise good work, or the winning of a scholarship to Oxford or Cambridge, by announcing an extra half-holiday.

One can imagine the impact of this tall, commanding figure on the first morning of September 1828, when he faced his new Sixth Form in the galleried Upper Bench Room for the first time. Arnold chose an ordinary kitchen chair for himself, and a small table as used by the pupils. His aim was not so much to impress as to watch, as he had at Laleham, for interest: his wish was to encourage and inspire. In one history lesson he told the story of "Old Parr", a certain ancient Shropshire farm labourer who lived through no less than ten reigns, from Edward the Fourth to Charles the First, achieving the great age of 152. The boys were required not to learn by heart but to think, and to describe the scenes the old man would have witnessed during the course of so long a life. This was very different from the teaching of history by dates and reigns: indeed, the subject of "modern" history itself was an innovation, and the desired result - a thoughtful essay written in good plain English - very different from the formal compositions of the past.

40

Arnold prefaced every lesson with a prayer before beginning his questioning of the boys, telling the pupil after each answer a quiet "That will do" or occasionally rewarding an intelligent reply with an approving "Clearly". Any outstanding answer would, we are told by one of his prefects, be met with a smile "which seemed worth more to me than all my trouble." Moreover Arnold himself was not above improving his own knowledge. He taught himself German but was not very convinced of his own pronunciation, and on more than one occasion would ask a boy to read the German text out loud, acknowledging his reading with a formal bow. Any boy who offended was sent out of the room before Arnold lost his temper, and was, on his return, duly forgiven: though there were times, as the years went by, when even Arnold's temper got completely out of control!

At first the hard work expected from his pupils resulted in fatigue, and more than one boy had to retire to the sick room to recuperate; but Arnold himself rarely complained. Indeed "I feel as if I could dictate to twenty secretaries at once!" he was heard to remark at the end of a busy day. Yet there is no doubt that his teaching was appreciated, however hard his students worked. "He taught us," said an old pupil later, "how to think."

Arnold himself, however, saw a great need for improvement. The standards of the school, as they appeared to him over those first years, seemed far below those even of his little school at Laleham. "I am daily more and more struck with the very low average of intellectual power of the boys at Rugby," he wrote in the February of 1831, after more than two years of teaching. All the same, he put all his efforts into the work he had taken on, and in due course was rewarded. "There is always a melancholy feeling," he wrote," in seeing the last sheaf carried of a good harvest - for who knows what may be the crop of the next year?"

Another innovation which Arnold brought about was to concentrate the boarders into houses, each with its own permanent housemaster, who would take an individual interest in the boys under his care. Thus, as an old pupil was to observe, every house was, as it were, an epitome of the whole school. "Every housemaster," as Arnold himself was to put it, "each had a horse of his own to ride." This was something new in education: a housemaster, usually with a family, providing not only a homely atmosphere but a sense of belonging to every boy. In addition, the salary of each master was significantly raised. This enabled them all, whilst they were still clerics, as was expected in those days, to be less dependent on their benefices and devote themselves more wholeheartedly to teaching.   But it was largely through his sermons that Arnold influenced the boys in his charge. Nearly every pupil took away with him the memory of those famous Sunday sermons, carefully prepared in words that the pupils could understand, and delivered with a solemnity that went straight to their hearts. "The tall valiant form," wrote Thomas Hughes, an ex-pupil, "the kindling eye, the voice, now soft as the low tones of the flute, now clear and stirring as the call of the Light Infantry bugle - all these things left a mark on the hearers, never to be forgotten. We listened, as all boys in their moods will listen (ay, and men too, for the matter of that) to a man whom we felt to be, with all his heart and soul and strength, striving against whatever was mean and unmanly and unrighteous in our little world."

It was the Christian nature of this famous school which Arnold prized the most. To be a Christian gentleman was the ideal. "It is not necessary," Arnold wrote, "that this should be a school of 300 or 100 or fifty boys, but it is necessary that it should be a school of Christian gentlemen." And in truth, this is what followed. "It soon began to be a matter of observation to us at the university," wrote Thomas Hughes, "that his pupils brought quite a different character with them to Oxford than that which we knew elsewhere - manly minded, conscious of duty and obligation, influence for good."

And indeed Arnold not only taught, but learnt to love the pupils whom he had watched growing up under his care - especially the senior lads. "I enjoy," he wrote in 1831, "and do enjoy, the society of youths of 17 or 18, for they are all alive in limbs and spirits indeed."

In fact, Thomas Arnold had now come to be sure of his vocation. Not the priesthood, for he still had doubts, but teaching, was to be his chosen way of life. Teaching chimed with all that was best and most inspiring in his world: a teacher who always remained a learner as well. "A teacher," he once declared, "should always be eager to experiment and to find out new things," an aim to which he aspired for the whole of his life.

Chapter 5   The Doctor in Trouble

THE GOOD DOCTOR OF RUGBY, however successful he had proved himself by reorganising a declining school, was not without his critics. The chief reason for this was his dogged determination to pursue his own line of religious thought, regardless of its consequences. Long ago he had had doubts about the nature of the Trinity, and although he had now been admitted to the priesthood, as befitted the headmaster of an ancient school, he was not afraid to voice his opinions.

His aim was what he called "Christian reform", which he preached weekly in the school chapel and later published freely in book form, along with volumes on the Classic writers and on Roman history. These offended many, including the "Sheffield Courier" which suspected him of socialist principles. "I care not for one party or another", he had declared, "but I do care for the country." Disgusted, Arnold decided to give up newspapers: "It only vexes me to read," he averred, "especially when I cannot do anything about it by writing."

Yet he was constantly criticising both politicians and priests, thereby losing all hope of ever becoming a bishop: "I regard with unabated horror the Conservatives, both in Church and State," he wrote, "and I marvel at the lethargy of the English nation. The people are never aroused from their Conservatism till mustard poultices are put to their feet!"

As for the Church, as he found it, Arnold did not mince his words. "When I think of the Church," he confided to his diary, "I could sit down and pine and die!"

In one lengthy letter to a friend, he wrote: "From the earliest period that I ever thought things I have had a strong sense of the exaggeration of the praises lavished upon the Church of England," going on to describe in detail the conduct of the Church of England from the time of Henry VIII "down to this actual moment - which has made it impossible for me to regard it with affection or esteem." "All Christians," he continued, "(with the exception, it may be said, of the Unitarians) hold in common the great foundation of Christian faith... but the relation between minister and people has become to my mind too like that of Priest and People - of Teacher and Taught exclusively, of Shepherd and Sheep - losing sight of that other relation which is so peculiarly Christian, that ministers and people are joint members of one society, Christ the true Shepherd, the only Priest, and the Holy Ghost, the great common teacher of all Christians.

"The Cathedral service is to some minds a most effectual help to devotion: to others it is a perpetual offensiveness... but is it all sufficient for all persons at all times, so that no variation from it should be tolerated? It should be simply like the different homes, different habits, and different tastes of any half-dozen Christian families in common life... The fault is in those who expect their neighbour to conform to their practice and take it amiss in him if he follows one that suits him better."

And again he insists that "ministers should be rather elder brothers, to my view, than fathers...As a young man thinking seriously about life, all this stuff about the true church would never so much as come into his head! He would feel and see that the matter of his soul's salvation lay between God and Christ on the one hand, and himself on the other, and that his belonging to this or that church had really no more to do with the matter than his being born in France or England, in Westmorland or in Warwickshire. The Scripture notion of the Church is that religious society should help a man to become better and holier, just as civil society helps him in civilisation."

Harsh words, perhaps, but worse was to come. Arnold was ready to transfer his allegiance to the good John Bunyan: he averred that he rated John Bunyan "to have been a man of considerably greater genius than any Pope or Bishop... His "Pilgrim's Progress" seems to be a complete reflection of Scripture, with none of the rubbish of the theologians mixed up with it."

Rubbish? After all those sermons of his in Rugby chapel? Rugby's Headmaster had really set the cat among the pigeons! Not content with this, he went on to label the ministers of established religion as "on the whole lethargic, arrogant, too Tory-minded" and insisted that a change of heart was needed - a universal church, perhaps. He even suggested that the ordinary parish church might well be shared by all denominations, with the various creeds conducting their individual services at different times of the day.

Arnold now found himself even supporting Catholic Emancipation - though no Catholic himself, knowingly upsetting his own prospects of promotion - and, when sending Susanna a copy of one of his pamphlets, joked: "Do you not think that I should be a queer Bishop and that the pamphlet is a queer way of wishing preferment?" He even worried his poor wife with the vehemence of his pronouncements. Although his controversial pamphlet had sold out in a few weeks, Mary confided to her diary that it was "occupying the minds of all, creating sensations of hope and fear, joy and grief, which perhaps no political question ever excited in so great a degree".

These were weeks of open warfare, which did no good to the Headmaster's reputation. The "Sheffield Courier" above all took him to task, and even his old friend John Keble, godfather to Arnold's son Matt, took offence at such views, introducing what was to become one of the most violent subjects of the time, Catholic Emancipation. Sadly, so divided on such an important issue, the friendship between Arnold and Keble was never quite the same again. Nevertheless Arnold persisted in his views, although he knew at the time of writing to Susanna that such apparent heresy would prove a permanent obstacle to any hopes he had of a bishopric.

By this time reports of Arnold's views had already alienated the papers of the day. The "Edinburgh Review" in particular was horrified that an influential man like the Headmaster of a famous school should have openly declared such an opinion. Some even criticised his mien in his own school chapel "with a face white with suppressed emotion, while the ring of his voice was indignant against injustice" - a comment which very nearly cost him his headmastership. A man in his position who was openly "teaching his own revolutionary views on both religion and politics to the boys of Rugby" could hardly expect to continue in education.

To which accusation Arnold replied with fervour: "I never disguise or repress my opinions, I have been, and am, most religiously careful not to influence my boys with them."

Even his old friend Coleridge was now becoming concerned about the Headmaster of Rugby. He was giving too much time to controversy and not enough to school matters. To which comment Arnold replied, deeply hurt: "I can truly say that I live for the school", adding: "I am sure that the more active my mind is, and the more it works upon great moral and political points, the better for the school."

But by 1836 the situation was becoming acute. Parents were now withdrawing their sons from the school; numbers were falling seriously, and resulted in the raising of fees. Two years later "John Bull" was investigating rumours of an expulsion, reflecting badly on Rugby's reformed prefectorial system. Three young prefects had been discovered pummelling a young fag's head against a wall and beating him with "a knotted blackthorn stick of unusual size. "Those young gentlemen ought to be openly stigmatised!" thundered the paper.

It turned out, on the evidence of another pupil, Clough, that the fag had disobeyed a prefect and was resisting lawful punishment. Two other prefects had been called in to help the first, the stick had been broken, and the fag's head accidentally banged against the wall. When none of them could cope any longer with such resistance, they reported him to their headmaster, who sent for the wrongdoer and on his confession expelled him on the spot. Furthermore Arnold actually rang the bell and ordered a chaise to send the boy back to his parents.

This incident, reported wildly, drove Arnold to fury, insinuating as it did that his version of the prefect system was at fault. Arnold himself knew the truth: that he must at all costs uphold the authority of his prefects.

The fag was in the wrong and the fag must be punished. Naturally it did seem as though Arnold had for once lost his sense of proportion, but the papers made the most of the incident, retaliating with rumours - completely untrue - of the prefects at Rugby being allowed to beat their juniors with canes "loaded with lead". It must have seemed to Arnold and Mary that their whole life and work was being jeopardised - by the Press as well as the clergy. But in this case Arnold stuck to his guns. He knew his own mind, and he knew his own school, and would brook no interference. He trusted his prefects and nothing would make him let them down.

Actually it later appeared that Arnold's judgment had been hasty. The chaise had put out its only passenger late at night and far from home, and the lad had had to make the rest of the journey on foot, not reaching his parents until the following morning. This had certainly not been Arnold's intention, but it did not resound to his credit. Fortunately in this case the Trustees still retained their belief in the headmaster they had appointed, and even went so far as to issue a public statement expressing their "entire satisfaction" with Arnold, praising his "most humane and liberal principles".

For the time being, then, he was safe from persecution. His old friend Coleridge, indeed, wanted him to sue the Press for libel, but this Arnold declined to do. "A life of peace," he said, "is one of the things which I vainly sigh for!"

He was conscious, however, of the approval of others in high places. He was offered, and refused, a stall in Bristol Cathedral, together with an annual income of £600, and also a fellowship at the newly-formed

46

London University, but this also he turned down, agreeing, however, to be one of the examiners in Arts. Of the new university he wholly approved: it was, he averred, "a great experiment", giving for the first time degrees to "Jews and heathens of all sorts", as it was quaintly put: moreover, examinations in the Scriptures should be voluntary, and certificates awarded to all who passed. This, he considered, was better than nothing - although a few years later he decided to resign his fellowship.

Meanwhile his school prospered, in spite of falling numbers. The prefects all held him in great esteem, some being even in tears, it is said, when the time came to leave the school. Arnold himself referred to these partings as between "father and son". "It is delightful to me," he once said, "to find how glad all the better boys are to come back here after they have left, and how much they seem to enjoy staying with me." Indeed, where the boys from other public schools seemed only too pleased to leave schooldays behind them, Arnold's pupils continued to write to and call upon him whenever possible. The humanity of their old headmaster often remained in their memory for life.

Indeed, one old scholar wrote of him that "he seems to be of so much use here that one would hardly like to see him elsewhere - excepting always the Regius Professor at Oxford" - a status which he did later acquire, as Professor of Modern History.

By 1838 most of the opposition had weakened, and Arnold was able to apply himself to his school in earnest. The trustees had even issued a second statement in which they emphasised their perfect trust in him. The school, as he often said, was his life, and nothing should interfere with it. Little did he know then that his own life was slowly coming to a close.

By now the school was flourishing again, and quite a few innovations had been introduced. There was a school magazine edited entirely by the boys, promising serious contributions both in prose and poetry, and evading all controversial subjects such as politics. A Debating Society had also been introduced, unlike so many such societies which tended to uproar, with everyone talking at once: each boy now had to stand up and speak clearly, with no interruptions. In addition a lively Dramatic Society had also been established, reminiscent of Arnold's boyhood and the dramatic productions of his own family in their Lakeland holiday home. Arnold and Mary were always present on such occasions and clapped and listened with the rest. Sheridan's "Rivals" in particular made its mark on the audience, both young and old, and one boy who took his part so seriously that he burst into tears, was rewarded by an invitation to the School House for breakfast with the family the following morning.

Sports, however, were still left, as in most schools, unorganised, though Arnold would occasionally stroll over to watch the boys at play. Football was still a group game with vast numbers of players, but Arnold had his own sons taught cricket, and always encouraged physical exercise in other spheres. On Sundays Arnold and his wife would take a walk around the school grounds, watching the boys amusing themselves and talking informally to anyone who wished. In the school sanatorium, too, both Arnold and Mary were daily visitors, playing "Beggar my Neighbour" with the convalescents and sitting informally by the bedside of those who were ill. More than one patient spoke, in later years, of the way that Mary "did everything her kind heart could suggest to amuse us, for which I shall ever bless her, dear kind lady." Their visits always closed with a prayer, sometimes written by Arnold himself, offering "time to think how we are passing our life".

By now all the old-fashioned lodging-houses had been replaced by eight official Houses in the care of enthusiastic housemasters who took a fatherly interest in their pupils. Indeed they once went so far as to come to the aid of a boy by the name of Henry Hatch, who was about to sit the Oxford entrance examination but was not in good health and already worried because his parents could not afford the fees. Housemasters and Headmaster together decided to raise a private fund for this purpose, and wrote to Henry's mother offering an exhibition for four years of, perhaps forty pounds a year, to save him from having to work for the examination, "which, we are sure, would, in his present state of health, be very injurious to him." Poor Henry, unhappily, died before the end of that year.

Arnold also made clear his view of the qualities he required of his masters: "A teacher should always be eager to experiment and to find out new things" - a view not previously taken by schoolmasters of the time, certainly not by old Doctor Wool. In making these suggestions he did not spare himself. "A teacher should leave after fifteen years," he often said, adding sometimes "or when you feel no emotion on receiving a new boy."

These were by no means the only changes made by Arnold as the years went by: changes which soon proved effective, and indeed were largely adopted by public schools, existing, with modifications, right up to the present day.

One such, suggested by Arnold in a letter to Dr Longley at Harrow, was that the two existing terms, Long Half and Short Half, might give way to three terms a year: as it was, Arnold considered the old arrangement "too wearying". Another was that standard Latin and Greek textbooks should be issued, written by teachers themselves; and a third, a plea for more co-ordination between public school headmasters on various issues (a forerunner of the modern Headmasters' Conference) to study such issues as fagging, bullying and expulsion. Certainly, some boys had had to be expelled from Rugby by Arnold himself, but he did it for good reasons, and later he was able to say with some satisfaction: "I never knew the school more free from positive evil."

A further step towards the school as he wanted it was the introduction of services of Confirmation, the first being held by the Bishop of Worcester, and continuing at least once every two years. Never before, Arnold averred, had there been so large a number of communicants. One of his pupils, Gover, later to become Canon Gover, who had previously been at Shrewsbury, comparing the two headmasters, said that his own late headmaster had "cared only for scholarship, little for morals " - which could certainly not apply to Arnold. One head, it seemed, had assembled some 70 of the cleverest boys into one House and concentrated on them alone: "an admirable device for winning Porson prizes and other university distinctions, but purchased at the wholesale sacrifice of moral good for almost four-fifths of the school, and the inculcation of a pagan selfishness for the favoured few." Such could never be the case under Arnold. Another pupil from Shrewsbury was astonished, on entering Rugby, to find boys "wandering about meadows without interruption from local farmers", which would certainly not have been approved of in the old days of riotous behaviour. The Shrewsbury boys, it appeared, still "plundered the orchards" and were hated by the countrymen. It was not surprising that the reputation of Rugby had begun to soar.

A further advantage accruing to Rugby at this time was the extension of the railway line, when on September 17th 1838 the first train from London drew in to the local station. There was no need, from now on, to rely on stage coaches and chaises to bring new pupils to the famous school: parents from a wide area immediately put down their sons' names for Rugby. By this time, on the domestic side, Arnold's own sisters, Lydia and Patty, both of whom had recently lost their husbands, had come to live in the district with their families. Frances had sent her two sons to the school in the care of her brother, and three of Arnold's own children, Matt, Thomas and Edward, were pupils already.

Altogether, Arnold, though still arousing controversy, both private and public, by his freedom of speech, was already making his name. For the next few years, in addition, Rugby was able to record a number of academic successes, which increased the confidence of parents.

In a wider field, also, the fame of the Doctor and his lady was spreading. Both were very conscious of the conditions of the society around them: together they visited the poor, and at one point consulted both Carlyle and Coleridge as to whether better living conditions could be brought about by some public effort. Coleridge, in reply, pointed out that "Do not most societies ... turn out very soon to be rather empty things, swollen mostly with cant, vanity and wind - the main reality in them - the dinners they eat?" Carlyle advised him to "canvass it further in your own thoughts and with others", shrewdly adding that he himself possessed "little money and little health." Meanwhile Arnold was close to becoming a public hero. His published sermons were admired, even by his enemies, and by his example it seemed as though, after all the previous troubles his place in the educational field was more secure than it had ever been before.

What perhaps crowned his success at Rugby was the visit of Queen Adelaide, widow of William IV. We have his eldest daughter Jane's description of this quite exceptional occasion: "She came in her chariot with her equipage and outriders" and was received by Arnold and the masters at the School House, going on to examine the school buildings "where the young gentlemen of this establishment uttered acclamations of joy!"

The Queen then expressed a somewhat unexpected wish to see the boys play football - "a fearful thing," wrote one of the players later, "for thin boots, swell trousers and a treacherous November soil" made rough outdoor play difficult. Their waistcoats having hurriedly been hung on the palings, "we presented anything but our usual martial appearance, arrayed in white trousers, belts and velvet caps. We looked, in fact, more like a mob of Cockneys on what might be their first introduction to the game!"

At this time football was played with vast numbers on each side. However the boys did their best, bringing in 75 from the School House and 225 from the rest of the school - a battle indeed, with Thomas Hughes (later to write the famous "Schooldays") included in the game, alongside Samuel Sanders, the boy who had once been complimented by Arnold on his acting. School House won both goals, in spite of their numbers, "and," wrote the recorder, "I felt proud of it, for Arnold and Queen Adelaide were looking on!"

Arnold's nine children were all gathered together on the steps to watch the Queen's return from the Close. The Queen's carriages were awaiting her here, and Jane reported later that Her Majesty "noticed them very kindly". Jane, the artist of the family, was later able to make sketches of this very special occasion, whilst Tom Hughes' description of the famous football match was to make the game of Rugby football known to all the world.

The following year Arnold himself was presented to the Queen, his diary on this occasion simply noting "I was amused by the novelty of the scene!"

Indeed, by this time, others were noticing and admiring the School, and there was even a prototype set up in Australia, of which Arnold was offered the headship, with the rider that he might well become "father of the education of a wide quarter of the globe!" Arnold proved interested, but decided that the role was not for him.

Apart from this offer, Arnold was quite partial to the idea of colonisation, and even considered briefly the possibility of emigration. "If we are alive fifteen years hence," he wrote to a missionary friend, "I think I would go with you gladly if they will make me schoolmaster there... No words can tell of the evil of such colonies as we have hitherto planted", with reference to the transportation of criminals there. When a certain John Gell had established a school of his own in Van Diemen's Land, Arnold had even given thought to buying land in the Swan River district, "that I may have my estate and the school buildings got into due order before I shut up shop at Rugby." He still held to his principle of limiting his headship to fifteen years, considering that was quite enough for the same headmaster to cope with. But it was not to be.

As it was, he inclined to the view that sending offenders to Australia was the worst thing possible for our Empire. The Government, he considered, would do better to send boys from good class homes, who could not profit from a university education, to make the best of themselves overseas: boys carefully selected, of course, certainly not the idle and indulgent. "I would far rather send a boy to Van Diemen's Land, where he must work for his bread, than send him to Oxford to live in luxury, without any desire of his mind to avail himself of his advantage."

Indeed, at one point he had thought of sending his own sons, Matt and Thomas, out to one of the colonies. "My sons," he said regretfully, "do not work as they should." Only Jane, his eldest, seemed "responsible", as he put it. At eighteen she had become his private secretary. Not that Arnold did not love all his children; but he often confessed himself unable to cope with Matt and Tom. "Very thoughtless and boyish," he called them. "I know not how to deal with it."

Matt and Tom by this time had both reached the Sixth Form, but seemed unable to settle down. "I do not see how the sources of deep thought are to be reached in him," wrote Arnold of Matt. "Matt likes general society and flitters about from flower to flower, but is not able to fix." Yet Arnold's worries were in the event to prove quite wrong. Matt, lazy as he had seemed, eventually won a scholarship to Balliol College, Oxford. "The news actually filled me with astonishment," his father wrote, adding "I have great hopes that success will act wholesomely on him." A strange remark concerning a youth who was later to become one of the most famous poets of his time!

By now the Headmaster of Rugby had well and truly vindicated himself. Not one of his enemies could stand up against him. His fortunes, too, had turned out favourably. Gone were the financial worries which he had so gladly and willingly shared with Mary. He had now bought land in Australia and New Zealand and invested in the new railway companies, taken out a £5000 insurance policy, and was the proud possessor of a holiday home in the Lakes.

He was now in a position to hand over responsibility for the School House to one of his masters. This now consisted of 61 boys, Thomas Hughes amongst them. In fact it was Hughes who in the brief span of 14 hours wrote to his headmaster on his announcement of his retirement from the School House: "Sir: We, the undersigned, have heard with regret your intention of giving up the School House. We venture to say that the personal regret we feel for you would make us extremely lament your leaving us, and we humbly hope that this expression of our feelings may be allowed some weight in influencing your determination."

This unusual epistle did succeed in Arnold's remaining at the School House for a further spell, but he was most unwilling to stay beyond his fixed period of fifteen years, for the sake of the School as well as himself. However, Matt's scholarship had impressed him. "So long as I can still run up the library stairs," he averred, he would remain; and if Thomas could follow his brother's example, he would be content.

Most of all, the epistle from the School House had revealed to him how much his work was valued. "What gives me pleasure to observe," he wrote, "is a steady and a kindly feeling in the school in general, towards the masters and towards each other."

A little later, he was to add: "The School jogs on in great tranquillity. All things are quiet and unexciting, the happiest state of mortal existence, and which it would be impossible for me ever to attain if I did not banish all newspapers, reviews, magazines and the like - so that when our immediate horizon is clear, I am not disturbed by the knowledge or consciousness of clouds elsewhere."

Certainly it seemed as though the clouds had rolled away. Not only was Arnold now fully recognised in his chosen vocation, but he was having honours heaped upon him. Rugby now being under five hours from London, boys from the south were coming to the school, and by March 1841 he was able to record that numbers had built up. "The school is very full - about 330 boys in all - quiet and well-disposed, I believe." Soon even this number was increased. In May of the same year "We are very full, fuller than ever, having more than 350 and nearly 40 names on the waiting list for admission, so that I do not know what is to be done. The new masters are stirring men, and equal to their work, and I hear that the subscription for the re-making windows for the chapel is getting on briskly." And by the following April, "The school is very prosperous in all externals, and very numerous, having swelled insensibly beyond its limits up to about 370 boys."

In the spring of 1840 the Prime Minister, Lord Melbourne, had offered the post of Warden of Manchester University to Arnold, but he had refused it. Personal advancement, he said, did not interest him: not even a bishopric. "I neither expect it, nor should I like it," he replied, "as it would so sadly interfere with Fox How." He could not give up his beloved family home and remove elsewhere, taking his wife and children from their beloved Lakeland home.

Oxford, however, "the place to which I should have the strongest local affection of any in the world, next to the valley of the Rother," would have greatly appealed to him. "It vexes me," he wrote, "to be shut out from the very place where I fancy I could do most good."

In fact he did soon receive an offer - of an Oxford Professorship of Modern History, which he gladly accepted, provided that as long as he lived in Rugby he was allowed to forfeit his stipend and devote it to some worthy University cause, such as establishing a history scholarship.

"The best rule seems to be to me," he wrote to friends, "to lecture exactly as I should write for the world at large, not cautious nor hostile, not "shocking" men's opinion, never declining to speak the truth, however unpopular it would make me." As a result of this he left Rugby on December 2nd 1841, along with Mary, his wife, and Matthew, Stanley and Clough, to give his inaugural lecture, taking only one day off from school. This meant leaving at 5 on a winter's morning, and returning at 11 at night - and, typically, taking a batch of Sixth Form exercise books to correct on the journeys.

"The Regius Professor," Stanley wrote later, "who is distinguished from the rest by his scarlet robes, took his place under the English rostrum amid a burst of general applause." The audience's attention never flagged for a moment, and "I hope may be taken as the beginning of a new sphere of happiness and usefulness for him, and of a new influence at work upon the University." Early in the next year Arnold was to spend a fortnight in Oxford to give eight lectures, staying in a house in Beaumont Street.

Certainly, after the storms, the future looked bright.

Chapter 7 Fox How

"I MUST HAVE MY PLAYTIME," the Doctor of Rugby had often said. However hard he drove himself, he knew instinctively what many professional men fail to realise, that you cannot overdo your strength. Arnold had long ago realised that to spend his whole life in the service of boys without a break would do more harm than good. Moreover he had realised the same with his pupils. He worked them hard, but was quick to detect when they were "fagged", as he put it, and for his pupils as well as himself he realised that a very necessary part of education was relaxation.

Arnold and Mary had for some time felt that the dull plains of Rugby were not the scenes they would choose in which to spend the rest of their lives. They had come from the woods and streams of riverside Laleham to the soggy fields of the Midlands, and with a young growing family to consider - eventually nine children - they longed to spend their leisure in different surroundings. They had already made several visits to the Lakes, and there had met and made friends with William and Mary Wordsworth. Mary, they knew, loved children - the more the merrier- whilst William, like Arnold, enjoyed books and long walks, and was already a well-known poet. What better choice for a family holiday retreat than Lakeland, where the Wordsworths were only too ready to look out for a suitable house for them?

In the event, the Wordsworths found for him not a house, but a plot of land eminently suitable for a family home. Not far from Dove Cottage, Grasmere, where Wordsworth and his sister Dorothy were happily living, was a hillside site overlooking the lake, where the Arnold family could now afford to have their own home designed and built. Arnold wrote enthusiastically to the pair at Grasmere, and the pair, equally enthusiastically, replied. The view would be perfect; the site was embowered in trees, and Dove Cottage was just a stroll round the lake when they wanted to visit their friends. Other literary people were often in the Lakes: Coleridge spent much time with them at Grasmere, and though the journey was long from London, from Rugby it was not nearly so difficult. Dorothy herself, delighted at the prospect of a horde of children, promised to do all she and her brother could to supervise the building of Fox How, as it was called, including the furnishings and the arrival of the servants.

We have Dorothy's own account of the new house at Fox How as day by day she walked over to the other side of the lake to see how the building was getting on. Dorothy busied herself, as the work continued, in putting the finishing touches to her new friends' holiday home. The Arnold servants had already paid visits, "and," records Dorothy, "the housemaid says she likes the place better every time she goes to it." Dorothy, always thorough and anxious to please, went from room to room examining every detail - except for the garrets. They could wait. One day we find her hurrying home from Fox How to finish the house-warming present she has been making for Mary Arnold: a rug for the floor. The Doctor, arriving three days later with his brood, confided to his diary: "How we did walk about and enjoy ourselves!"

Later, he described the surroundings in winter-time. "The higher mountains that bound our view are all snow-capped, but it is all snug and warm and green in the valley. Nowhere on earth have I ever seen a spot of more perfect and enjoyable beauty, with not a single object not in tune with it, look which way I will. Close above us are the Wordsworths and we are in our own house, a party of 15 souls, so that we are in no danger of being dull, and I think it would be hard to say which of us all enjoys our quarters the more."

The house still stands, white against the encircling trees, with its view across to the lake to the village of Grasmere. It was from here that the visiting Wordsworths, taking their favourite chairs by the tall window, were wont to look out at the wonderful view while the various Arnold children played around the sitting-room.

For her part, Dorothy was delighted. She adored the Arnold children, "good and wild and happy as it is possible for children to be. Little Willy is such a funny thing... and Mary too is as queer as ever. Matt and Tom don't appear to me grown...Jane is sweet and gentle as ever....Edward the same clever thing."

The Doctor, for all his schoolmasterly ways, enjoyed himself to the full. Casting off his cares, he reminded himself that he was here to relax; "I must throw off my work altogether," he declared, and once again, "I must have my playtime." He romped, played and walked with his nine children, who all adored their father, "Pappy" as they called him. In turn he had his fun with them. For his own and their amusement he dubbed them his "small fry" or, quaintly, his "dogs", and delighted to watch, often to join in, their various exploits at different times of the year: sliding on frozen Rydal water, shooting snipe, walking on the mountains, taking with them a picnic lunch of oatcakes for all the family, bathing in summer, and, indoors, play-acting and composing charades, a favourite game with the Arnolds through at least two generations. Nevertheless the children had to follow a certain routine, holidays or no holidays.

Arnold thought out the house rules as seriously as he did the school time-table, and saw that these were properly displayed so that all the children could study them. But he brought to it all a touch of humour very much his own. His rules for his "Dogs" make interesting reading:

1　That all Dogs do observe hours: to wit, that they be downstairs to breakfast by half past eight o'clock, and in to dinner by 5 o'clock, and in the house to tea at 9 o'clock, not to go out again.

2　That dogs Didu (Edward) and Widu (William) do not fish nor go out rowing or sailing without a man, nor go on walks without the older Dogs.

3　That all Dogs, unless there is some public engagement, do stay within doors, and read for their canine education, from 10 o'clock to 12.

4　That all Dogs bear themselves reverently and discreetly towards Dog K (Jane, the eldest), not barking, biting or otherwise molesting her, under pain of heavy justice with many smites."

We still have the children's own records of those days, in the form of the "Fox How Magazine," with pen- and -ink illustrations by Jane. We see Mary skating on the ice and falling over, petticoats a-flutter; the family sitting-room, with the younger ones playing with a toy boat their father has made for them; a family picnic in summer-time; and the whole tribe crowded together on the landing-stage by the lakeside, the boys in top hats, the girls in flowing skirts, moments before the stage breaks down and pitches them all into the water. But we also have the record by at least one of the winter house-guests, snowbound indoors for several weeks, who tells a very different story: "The whole nine," he writes, "in the highest state of young, vigorous, turbulent life, were never out of the house for more than a few moments. I was often obliged to take refuge in my own room, but that was simply because my quiet tête-a-tête life makes it difficult to attend to anything in a crowd of bee-like, or ant-like, activity such as goes on in the drawing-room here!"

Other visitors may have felt the same at first, but they soon discovered the peculiar charm of Fox How and its distinguished Doctor. Arnold frequently invited his senior boys from Rugby to stay in the holidays "to refresh their health when they get knocked up by the work, and to show them mountains and dales: a great point in education, and a great desideratum to those who only know the central or southern counties of England" - an extraordinarily perceptive view of education for those times. He even invited one or two of those boys he had had to expel, bearing them no ill will, and understanding them as few grownups, even their own parents, ever could.

Another visitor who did not at first find Arnold to his liking was the diarist Henry Crabb Robinson, who on a visit to Rydal one Christmas went to church on Sunday, at which Arnold happened to be officiating. "He has the face and voice and manner of a man of talents," was Robinson's diary entry, "but his sermon was altogether cold - as bad as the morning itself: I sat shivering without my greatcoat." He may be forgiven for his hasty judgment, for the sermon was not the only source of cold: a village church can be icy in winter, especially when the listener has forgotten his coat.

However, on dining with the Arnolds a few days later, Robinson revised his opinion: "I like him more, the more I see of him." On another occasion when Robinson met the Doctor, he talked very amicably to him about the book Arnold had been engaged upon, his "History of Rome", and did in fact read the whole of the first volume the following day, admitting: "I now feel a strong interest in Roman history, which I never did before."

The two occasionally went walking together when Robinson was in the Lakes on holiday. Robinson was finding, as so many had found before him, that Arnold was a man who took some knowing. In time he became a welcome guest at Fox How, where the noisy children were fast growing up, and when in the summer of 1842 he heard of the Doctor's sudden and early death, he was amongst the first to be affected. "What a happy house at once broken up!" Robinson sighed, and immediately went to Fox How to call on poor Mrs Arnold, and "was consoled by finding her" not only able but willing to talk of the poor Doctor.

Perhaps the visitors who appreciated most the family home at Fox How were the lads who had not done well at school, but who were ready to profit from their Headmaster's unusual gift for understanding the nature of boyhood. To this was added the spontaneity with which the nine children received these ill-matched visitors, and the motherly affection displayed to them by the Doctor's wife Mary. Some of these lads had never known a mother's care, being despatched straight from home at an early age into the rough-and-tumble of school life. Others, as Arnold had already guessed, had outgrown boyhood altogether and had only got into trouble at school by the accident of their own rapidly maturing size and strength; whilst more than one schoolboy had found at Fox How the sympathy and understanding not granted him at home.

Arnold was well aware of this, and it is not surprising that so many of his old pupils, including George Hughes, expelled from the school, were able to pick up the threads of their lives again when visiting the very different "Head" of Fox How. Arnold, for sure, would have been glad to know that his beloved Lakeland home had benefited, not only his own children, but the boys whom he had in his care. For many years afterwards Fox How continued to be the family refuge for Mary and her children, but without the good Doctor and his beloved "Dogs" it could never be quite the same again.

Chapter 8   Last Days

THE YEAR 1842 began happily enough. Fox How for the holidays was now an accepted routine, and school affairs were going well. Arnold was enjoying his Professorship at Oxford, combining it with school duties. His doubts about his sons had largely disappeared, and the family was now rejoicing in the engagement of the eldest child, Jane, to George Cotton, an assistant master at Rugby. They were to be married in the summer.

Arnold was not, at first, impressed with his favourite daughter's choice of a husband. Worthy as he may have been, George was not prepossessing. "Hesitating and awkward gait," was her father's description, "slow in speech, somewhat slouching in figure, wore a monocle and fidgeting with it all the time."

All quite understandable, for a nervous young schoolmaster only too aware of the famous Head's opinion. But Jane was deeply in love with the awkward youth who so much admired her. A lively person herself, she was warm-hearted and tolerant, and when he proposed, receiving his future father-in-law's permission, George seemed happier than he had ever been. Perhaps a little encouragement was all he needed.

George had been a master at the school for several years, and could offer Jane a suitable home. But few thought him worthy of the Headmaster's daughter. Wordsworth, who met him occasionally, admitted that "he may be a very good young man and a clever one, but" (that "but" again!) "a more unattractive youth - but he is not like a youth - I never saw."

George, however, was made welcome, both to the Arnolds' drawing-room and to their holiday house at Fox How. At least, as Arnold admitted, he had the necessary "moral thoughtfulness", and that, perhaps, made up for his unfortunate manner. Arnold probably remembered his own young days, when he had not been much of a social success, and, as friends said, "took a great deal of knowing". Jane, however, was happy. Mary, too, began to like him, once she got used to his shyness. "How often," she wrote in her diary, "I find Mr Cotton's name amongst our guests!"

By 1841 George was an accepted member of the household, happy in the knowledge that Jane had now been engaged to him for a year. The wedding had been fixed for June, and plans formed for an outdoor reception, in lovely summer weather, in the Arnolds' private garden at Rugby. And then the blow fell.

In May George had to admit that his attraction to Jane had been romance, not love. He felt unable to go on with the wedding.

One feels sad that such a situation, so near to the marriage date, should have arisen, but at least George had the courage to withdraw. The news came as a shock to all the Arnold family, but poor Jane was completely devastated.

She sank into a depression, from which nothing that Thomas or Mary could say seemed able to lift her. But the blow for Arnold was too sudden. He was devoted to his eldest daughter, his private secretary as well as his future son-in-law, and all their plans had gone awry. On May 17th he suffered a sudden collapse whilst out walking with his wife, and by Trinity Sunday, May 22nd, he was confiding to his diary: "I write this in my bedroom during morning service, having been for the last 4 or 5 days unwell and confined to my room: a slight feverish attack having been brought on by my distress and anxiety about dearest Jane.

May I dare to hope that God has blessed this great trouble to me by having made it the means of softening my heart? I am now within a few weeks of completing my 47th year. Am I not old enough to contemplate steadily its end - what it is coming to and must come to? What is it to live unto God? May God open my eyes."

It was a cry for help unusual from such a man.

He appeared to be recovering, and by the Thursday he could write: "I am mercifully restored to my health and strength. Tomorrow I hope to be able to resume my usual duties. Now then is the dangerous moment lest I should fall into my old hardness. Gracious Father, keep me now through Thy Holy Spirit; keep my heart soft and tender now in health and amidst the bustle of the world!"

A hard prayer to say: all but blaming himself for the disaster that had come upon Jane. But he regretted the "hardness"; at all times, even in distress, he could not but speak the truth.

The next morning he was back at school as usual, "but so weak as to be unable to do all my regular work, and altogether incapable of hard reading or writing."

To Mary he confided that he felt "quite a rush of love to God and Christ", and that he hoped he should be "softer and more gentle". To Mary he promised that he would remain in his study in the evening, writing something "to keep his heart tender", as Mary wrote in her diary, "for this seemed his overflowing desire." Not only was he sad for Jane, but reproachful to himself for his hard feelings towards the young man of her choice. This was a situation he had not met before, and it was difficult to forgive himself.

Mary was aware of the situation in the husband she loved. "There is something of softness and love which I cannot describe," she confided to her diary, "in his whole manner and conversation. I have even seen him watching himself and recalling words if he thought they could be felt in the least degree unkindly."

Indeed the successful Headmaster of Rugby was suffering as he never had before.

At Fox How that summer Arnold kept his diary faithfully for the whole of June and well into July that year, writing each night of his hopes and despair: "I do feel anxious to do God's service, but yet how many faults beset my wish to serve God - how mixed are the motives, how feeble the execution!" The words of a sick and troubled man. On May 1st he was writing: "Another day and another month ended. I would wish to try to keep a watch over my tongue, as to vehement speaking, and censuring others" - George, surely, in particular- "and of going down the hill of life, and having done far less than half my work."

On June 6th he was writing: "I have been just looking over a newspaper - so much sin and so much suffering in the world are there displayed, and no-one seems able to remedy either. And then the thought of my own private life so full of comforts is very startling when I contrast it with the lot of millions, whose portion is so full of distress or of trouble! May I be kept humble and zealous!"

By now he was feeling a little better. "I have felt better and stronger all this day, and I thank God for it - but may He keep my heart tender, and save me from becoming hard and careless as I grow stronger. May He keep me gentle and patient, yet active and zealous!"

On Saturday June 11th Arnold wrote: "The day after tomorrow will be my birthday, if I am permitted to live to see it. My 47th birthday since my birth -how large a portion of that life which I am to pass on earth! And then? What is to follow this life? How visibly my outward work seems contracting and softening away into the gentler employments of old age! In one sense, how nearly can I now say "Vixi"? And I thank God that as far as ambition is concerned, it is, I trust, mortified fully. I have no desire other than to step back gradually from my place in the world, and not to rise to a higher one. And yet there are works which I would do with God's permission before the night cometh. And that great work if I might be permitted to take part in it. But let me above all mind my own personal work, to keep myself pure and zealous and believing, labouring to do God's will but not anxious that it should be done by me rather than by others, if God disapproves of my doing it."

Arnold's last words were spoken that June afternoon in 1842, after he had been out walking with Mary. "I remember his earnest admiration of the depth of blue in the sky, " she wrote later. The two of them wandered about their private garden for a while, "and his conversation had never more depth and yet more gentleness."

Mary retired to bed that night, leaving her husband in his study, preparing a sermon for the next day, Sunday, as well as making up his nightly journal. They had prayed together in the bedroom, as was their custom, using a prayer that he had composed the year before whilst at Fox How. When he finally retired to bed, he seemed better and more at peace with the world than before.

Just before 5 o'clock he woke in pain, and Mary, already anxious, suspected angina pectoris. She called the servant, Elizabeth, to come immediately. Later, as Mary was dressing, it seemed to the watchers that Thomas was muttering a prayer. A doctor was sent for, and a prayer was said for him. Mary read him the 51st Psalm and other verses. Meanwhile Elizabeth prepared the brandy and hot flannels, hot water bottles and mustard poultices which were customary at the time. Arnold, outspoken as ever, asked the doctor to tell him the truth, and was told that, like his father long ago, he was suffering, as suspected, from angina pectoris. To his son, Arnold said: "My son, thank God for me. I have suffered so little pain in my life that I feel it is very good for me. I do so thank God for giving me this pain."

The doctor, on a return visit, expressed the opinion that his patient would recover, and accordingly Mary went downstairs for a moment, leaving a servant with him, but was soon recalled as her husband was now unconscious. She summoned the other children who were at home, and the family prayed together at the bedside, until at last their father died - just twenty-four hours short of his 47th birthday. He was buried in the vault of the School chapel, where he had so often preached to his boys, and both boys and masters were throughout in tears.

But Thomas Arnold, seemingly in the prime of life, had finished his great work. He had come to an ancient school and reversed its fortunes, even though he had never expected to become a teacher at all; and he probably performed a better service to education than he ever would have as a priest. He had come a long way from those early days at Cowes when he learnt his lessons by the quayside watching the ships arrive from foreign lands, and with his aunt who taught him with her geography cards and sent him pocket money at school.

But these things had remained with him, and made his teaching fresh and memorable. Nor had he judged his pupils on their scholastic results. His aim had ever been, first to produce true Christians, secondly to turn out English gentlemen, and thirdly, to educate hard-working honest men who would never forget the principles he taught them.

Indeed, the reformed Rugby was fast becoming a pattern for other schools. Just a year before, Cheltenham College had been founded, followed in time by Marlborough, Wellington, Rossall and Clifton, all pursuing what had now become the modern methods. Arnold's old headmaster at Winchester, Dr Moberley, wrote: "A more singular and striking change has come upon our public schools: a change too great for any person to appreciate who has not known them in both these times."

George Cotton, who had caused the Arnolds such unhappiness, went on to become Headmaster of Marlborough and eventually a bishop. Whether his unfortunate manner was to change is not recorded, but he did at last achieve a position of which his old Headmaster would have approved. George's wife too approved of Arnold's views on education, and recorded that Arnold's prefect system had decided her new husband to apply the same principles to his own Sixth Form. George in turn expressed his admiration of the man who so nearly became his father-in-law, saying that he "threw himself with his whole heart" into the school he took over. No better tribute could have been paid his former headmaster.

Amongst Arnold's children, Matt, over whom his father had worried so much, eventually became a lay Inspector of Schools, apart from his popularity as one of the greatest poets of the Victorian age. Matt was sent all over the world to report on education - journeys of which his father would wholly approve - whilst his brother Thomas went out to help organise education in Tasmania.

Young Edward also became a Government Inspector of schools in Devon and Cornwall, whilst William rose to be the first Director of Public Instruction in the Punjab. The charming children whom Dorothy Wordsworth had dandled on her knee long ago had all turned out well.

And Jane? After the blow she had suffered, she continued valiantly with her own life. Eight years after the disappointment, she married the "boy next door", William Forster, who lived almost within sight of their beloved Fox How. Some twenty years later, it was William Forster who put through the first Elementary Education Bill, the beginning of universal education in the 1870's. Thomas Arnold's traditions had been well and truly handed on.

Jane's niece, the famous Mrs Humphrey Ward, seemed to sum up the whole of the Doctor's views on education. Mrs Ward was in the Ladies' Gallery of the House of Commons when Forster made his speech introducing the famous Bill. Let her sum up the life of the good Doctor of Rugby when she said: "It has always been clear to me that the scheme of the Bill was largely influenced by William Forster's wife (Jane Arnold) and through her by the conviction and beliefs of her father."

Nothing could have pleased the good Doctor of Rugby more than to have heard those words.

.oOo.

'The Reverend Francis Kilvert'

by Eileen Elias   *ISBN 1-902628-59-4*
Kilvert was a Victorian rural vicar whose life is revealed in this fascinating biography.

———

'John Constable - The Artist and the Man'

by Eileen Elias   *ISBN 1-902628-58-6*
Eileen Elias returns with another fascinating biography which captures the spirit of the times, the inspiration of the artist and the mood of the man.

———

Readers wishing to communicate with the author about these works, are advised in the first instance, to address their correspondence to Eileen Elias, c/o Pipers' Ash